THE TOP 10 REASONS

— THE —

RICH

GO BROKE

POWERFUL STORIES THAT WILL TRANSFORM YOUR FINANCIAL LIFE...**FOREVER**

THROUGH THE EYES OF ONE OF AMERICA'S TOP FINANCIAL PLANNERS

JOHN MACGREGOR, CFP®

Eleuthera Press

THE TOP 10 REASONS THE RICH GO BROKE

Published by Eleuthera Press, an imprint of RDA Press, LLC

RDA Press LLC
15170 N. Hayden Road
Scottsdale, AZ 85260
480-998-5400

First Eleuthra Press Edition: March 2020

ISBN: 978-1-947588-09-7

Printed in the United States of America

*My sincere appreciation to everyone
who supported me on this wild journey.
From the bottom of my heart, thank you.*

*Most importantly, thank you
to my late mom and my still-going-strong dad
for all your unconditional love and support.
You made this adventure possible.*

CONTENTS

PART THREE:
TIME TO TRANSFORM

DISCLAIMER

The stories in this book are based on true stories with real individuals. I've recreated events, locales, and conversations from my memories of them. To maintain anonymity, I've changed the names of individuals, places, and dates. I have also changed identifying characteristics and details such as physical properties, occupations, and places of residence.

Learning from your mistakes is smart;
learning from other people's mistakes is genius.

– Anonymous

Robert Kiyosaki
Best-selling author of *Rich Dad Poor Dad*

I have always believed that mistakes are opportunities to learn. And the best mistakes are the ones other people make – especially when you recognize them and learn from them.

I do not care for financial advisors.

If you have read any of my *Rich Dad* books, you already know that. It's not personal. I just don't believe that we get smarter by turning over decision-making responsibilities and control of our money to other people. And I have serious concerns about the financial industry as a whole – its lack of transparency and the way it makes its money.

Most of the financial advisors I have met are decent people. But it's important to know that their primary job is to sell you something. They are sales people. Very few have any real financial education or any interest in real financial education.

In the late 1970s and early 1980s, when 401(k)s first came on the market, many people switched careers to become financial advisors.

Schoolteachers, car salespeople, real estate agents, waiters and waitresses, and insurance agents were all taking training programs to become financial advisors and – in less than two months – they were "professional financial advisors" ready to plan your financial future by selling you financial products.

In 1975, my day job was working for Xerox. At night, I was taking courses to become a Certified Financial Planner™ (CFP®), an intensive, three-year program.

I did not complete the CFP® program. I am happy I went as far as I did because I learned a lot. I did not complete the CFP® program because I was more interested in real estate and in taking advanced real estate investment courses.

An important distinction – and what I did learn – was that financial advisors are like bookkeepers and that CFPs are like CPAs, Certified Public Accountants. This is an importance difference.

I am honored to write this Foreword for John MacGregor's book, for a number of reasons:

Reason #1: I asked John to write this book. The *Rich Dad* series of books needs content and teaching from someone with John's professional experience.

Reason #2: John is a Certified Financial Planner,™ but he is much more than a financial planner. He often instructs other CFPs and financial planners on this vital professional service.

Reason #3: I respect John. He is real and has dedicated his life to this important subject. He is a true professional… and a student of his profession. Whenever I have a question on financial planning, he is my "expert," my advisor on the very important world of financial planning.

Reason #4: Financial planning encompasses much more than just investing. Real financial planning is about life planning and estate planning. If you do not have plans in place, *first* your family has to deal with the mess you leave behind; *second*, if you leave anything behind, your family goes to war over your estate; and *third*, the government takes most of your estate, before your family gets anything.

Reason #5: John's book is not a text book. Text books are boring. John's book is a story book, a book of real-life, tragic financial horror stories – real horror stories that did not have to happen. This book is about helping you avoid making critical mistakes that can devastate you and your family's life.

Reason #6: John is a close and dear friend. Like me, he was raised in Hawaii and we both played rugby for the Hawaii Harlequin Rugby Club, at different times of course, due to the differences in our ages.

Reason #7: Humans learn from mistakes. As I've said: Sometimes the best mistakes are the mistakes of others, especially if we recognize them and use them as opportunities to learn. This book is essential for the financial library of anyone who is serious about their financial future.

These are the reasons why I asked John to write this book. John offers us a chance to learn from someone else's stupid mistakes, rather than make them ourselves – and suffer the financial consequences.

–Robert Kiyosaki

PART ONE

THE

TRAP

CHAPTER 1

Why I Wrote This Book

My name is John MacGregor and I've circled the entire financial industry for the better part of my adult life. In my earlier years, growing up and through college, I was a landscaper and later in life I sat in a large high-rise office. I've been on both sides of the financial line: the poor and the prosperous.

I've worked with countless individuals through the years, from those struggling to find financial footing to those deemed "well-off" by general society. In my experience, the level of wealth or income didn't matter because, in fact, *everyone* has the *exact* same problem when it comes to money. Most people today use money to dull their pain rather than fulfill their purpose.

> **Most people today use money to dull their pain rather than fulfill their purpose**

As a result, time and time again I've witnessed the financial despair far too many people face. It's a constant and desperate struggle to keep their heads above water.

And it's happening every day. Every. Single. Day.

Sometimes I'm fortunate enough to meet clients *before* they're caught in those traps, but that's rarely the case.

Usually I find people in the midst of some serious trouble. I would give them advice, guidance, and a ton of information, and although they'd enact the recommendations, within a short period of time they were back to making the same mistakes that got them in their mess in the first place. They'd be on the phone or in my office wondering why everything was still the same. No matter how much counseling I gave or how much planning we did together, despite their "absolute commitment" to the agreed upon plan, nothing changed. Quickly they were spiraling out of control once again and back to living a life of pain, stress and anxiety. They slipped back to living in a place I call "Pain Island."

It's enough to make you want to scream. And I certainly did on more than a few occasions.

After the dust would settle, I'd do what I was taught to do: dig in. I'd sift through their financial statements, expenditures, credit card statements, I'd see the withdrawals from their investment portfolio and invariably discover that they had slipped back into the same bad habits.

That's when I came to realize that information doesn't cause transformation.

Let me say that again: ***Information does not cause transformation.***

> **Information does not cause transformation.**

We have more information (and more access to it) than at any other time in history, but as a nation we are financially illiterate. This financial crisis is the greatest epidemic in our society, and it's affecting more people than all diseases combined.

What I later realized was that none of this is their fault. We've been programmed to fail financially.

I wrote this book to lay a new foundation for you, dear friend, and those who desperately want to crawl out from under the weight of their financial stress. It's an interesting journey and I ask you to bear with some background information first.

When you understand I'm a guide, a mentor who wants the best for you, I think you'll realize I'm not going to take you on a trip just for the sake of it; each destination, each word, each story has a purpose.

To help you.

These ten stories have the power to transform your life. As you read these stories, as you absorb their harsh realities, I want you to be introspective. I want you to share in their journeys and evaluate your own frame of mind. I want you to begin taking stock of your belief system and recognize there are traps set throughout your own life … and you probably never noticed most of them before.

It's like taking a nice hike in the woods, enjoying the beautiful weather and scenery, soaking in the freshness of the pines, feeling the leaves crunching beneath your feet, and not having a clue someone set a whole host of B.E.A.R. Traps all around you (more on that later). While you are walking in peaceful reverie, danger lurks with each step.

My ultimate goal for you is that you walk away with a greater sense of confidence that you *can* live abundantly and no longer stress about your finances as well as have a newfound awareness of the traps that are constantly lying in wait for the unsuspecting.

A WORTHY COMPANION

I highly encourage you to download the supplemental guidebook that accompanies *The Top 10 Reasons the Rich Go Broke*. It's available *completely FREE* at *www.johnmacgregor.net.*

This guidebook is *designed* to help you understand your financial views, history, beliefs, standing, and even literacy. As you work through this book and read the 10 stories about how wealthy people lost (or almost lost) everything they had acquired, the guidebook will provide opportunities for you to be reflective, to dig deeper, and perhaps connect more intimately to the people whose lives were forever changed.

The *most effective learning* happens when you're active in it. Reading is a passive activity. Like watching TV or a movie, aside from truly memorable characters or scenes, we often forget most of what we watch or read … *if* we're not engaged directly.

> ## The *most effective learning* happens when you're active in it.

When you truly value your financial life and health, you'll *desire* to take time to dig in deeper. This guidebook will help you do just that.

YOUR TURN

Take a moment now to visit the *Resource* section at johnmacgregor.net. There you can download your free guidebook. If you work best on paper, go ahead and print out a copy. Or consider having the digital file readily available on your laptop, tablet, or even a smartphone as you work through the book.

Be engaged. Be active. Dig deep. It's going to make a world of difference in the end. I promise.

CHAPTER 2

Cut to the Chase

You're about to embark on a journey unlike any financial book you've read. This journey you're about to take can have the power to transform your financial life so you can forever avoid and remove the destructive and painful traps you've been falling into all your life … those that have been wreaking havoc on you and your family.

I warn you, this book will elicit a lot of emotion, sadness, and resentment, and may even cause a tear or two. That's the point. In order for you to make the long-term changes necessary to not only survive in this world but, more importantly, to *thrive*, it must be emotional.

It's likely (if you're like most people) you've wondered how some people got rich. We may search for some "secret" only they know about.

But have you ever wondered how rich people go broke? Of course you have – it's why you're digging into this book. Whether it's about curiosity, a sense of satisfaction, or self-preservation, hearing stories about the rich losing everything has great appeal and power.

Unlike the success stories you've likely heard time and again, these stories offer an incredible opportunity to learn from other

Mistakes are where real and meaningful change occurs.

people's mistakes. Mistakes are where real and meaningful change occurs.

Success stories are easy. And cheap. There are plenty of them out there, but where real learning occurs is in the mistakes people make, the errors and stumbles and falls they took, because that gives us more clarity on what to avoid. When we recognize some of those same mistakes in our own lives, in our own patterns – if we're being honest with ourselves – we can learn, shift, and adjust as needed to avoid the same pitfalls and traps.

The stories contained in this book are personal. They concern people I know, people I've worked with closely. They provide a glimpse into the minds of highly successful people who lost almost everything (and in some cases *did* lose everything). Each story offers backstage access to why people of wealth go broke and why these lessons are vital for anyone looking to achieve and maintain financial peace and freedom.

Specific identifying details – such as names, locations, and dates – have been changed in order to protect the identities of these individuals. We'll keep the focus on the lessons contained within the stories rather than who these people are/were.

Although this book is about the rich, every story here contains critical insights that can save anyone from making the same devastating financial mistakes – mistakes you *will* face. How much money was lost in these stories doesn't matter. My goal is for you to focus on the lessons because each story offers ideas you can immediately apply to your everyday life.

There are specific reasons so many people (rich and poor) struggle financially. Yet, there is *one* that stands above all others. It boils down to one principle I've developed: B.E.A.R.

Hence, the *B.E.A.R. Trap.*

The B.E.A.R. Trap is a crippling internal weakness we all share. It lurks in the weeds waiting for us to wander by and stumble into its snap trigger. Once you understand this harmful, unfolding principle you unwittingly fight against every day, you will be able to release the power it has over you and finally begin the process of discovering and achieving the financial peace and freedom you deserve. This principle allows you to finally eliminate and avoid these pitfalls and the subsequent pain it washes over your life.

WHY MISTAKES?

I've worked with and counseled over 5,000 people and businesses over the past 25 years. The pain and frustration people have, regardless of their wealth, is real. I've seen it firsthand. And I've learned that it's the *mistakes* that matter most when it comes to genuine, beneficial learning and real change.

78% of people are living paycheck to paycheck

There are over 100,000 personal finance books promising financial stability, health, and well-being. And yet financial problems have only grown worse. When I started my new company four years ago, the number of full-time working adults in the U.S. living paycheck to paycheck was 73%. Today, it's 78%. That's *in spite* of the ever-growing quantity of financial advice available at our fingertips.

Most people readily admit they learn more from their mistakes than from lessons taught in school. But pick up just about any financial advice book and it'll be filled with stories of how people made money.

Not how they lost it.

We're bombarded with feel-good messages of prosperity in modern marketing, and we're derided as complete fools for the bad financial choices we make. Yet, how often do we take the time to actually sit down with some of the men and women who have "**been there, done that**"?

Every year people attempt to reach the top of Mt. Everest. Every year people die trying. While that's a tragedy, what would be more tragic is if no one bothered to understand *why* they died.

It's specifically because of those failures that others have a **better** chance of achieving their goals … but only if they pay attention to those lessons paid for at the highest price.

WHY STORIES?

My friend and mentor, Robert Kiyosaki, author of the international best-selling book *Rich Dad Poor Dad*, has always said, "There are two ways to share knowledge: You can push information in, or you can pull it in with story, because a good story well told can change the world."

I chose stories as a way to share this message because we connect through stories on an emotional level. Stories bring us together as we

WHAT YOU REMEMBER

HOW WE LEARN

90%

ACTIVE
Taking Action
Discussing
Journaling
Mentoring Others

PASSIVE
Listening
Watching
Reading

10%

feel empathy for one another, laugh together, and relate to someone else. Stories make a point. They deliver a concise message (when done well) and they do so in a memorable way.

What's fascinating is how the brain responds to stories. Countless research studies have determined that the brain reacts much differently to stories than it does, say, with facts and data. Emotional and personal stories engage the brain in a much greater manner and elicit the release of various brain chemicals such as dopamine and oxytocin. These chemicals and others force us to remember and learn at a much more accelerated rate than by simply reading a textbook or a traditional self-help book. The overarching conclusion indicates that the brain loves stories.

Stories tap into our imagination, requiring our active participation. When you read a story, *you* are the one bringing the setting and characters to life based on what you read. Your active involvement means you have an investment in it, too.

Figures and stats are clinical. They aren't emotionally charged or interesting enough to generate an emotional connection. They certainly have their place and can enhance a story's theme (its point), but by themselves they are dry and unmemorable.

People want to hear stories that are relatable and trigger feelings within them because stories also build connections. You relate to people you read about in stories, even if they're fictional, more than you will reading a clinical biography.

For over 27,000 years (the earliest dating of cave drawings), telling stories has been one of our most fundamental communication methods. Parables create simple, memorable mental images that audiences can easily connect with and discover the key meaning within. Children have values instilled through fairy tales and short stories with characters they can imagine. A well-written tale allows the reader the opportunity to build the scenes based on their own experiences and imaginations. That experience provides the reader a wonderful way to make these stories, and their lessons within, last in their memories longer.

Like most financial books crammed onto bookstore shelves, I could have simply listed the dos and don'ts or the whys behind how people went broke – but that would not be sufficient to create the emotional charge you need in your mind to make the lessons stick.

Stories instill images and meaning and explain how the world works.

Unlike the mountain of typical how-to personal finance books that use traditional methods (that rarely produce real change), these stories have the power to elicit something deep within that will then allow you to make meaningful transformation in your life.

It's clear that more information is not the answer. If it were, none of us would be financially stressed, overweight, smoking, or dealing with any number of vices. In other words, if information was all we needed to transform our life, we would all be rich, happy, and thin.

> **If information was all we needed to transform our life, we would all be rich, happy, and thin.**

We need more than information to change our behaviors and become the person we desire and deserve to be.

The stories in this book are based on true events. You'll follow people who enjoyed wealth, lived the "good life," and lost almost everything. Understanding where these people were coming from provides insight into the challenges they faced later on. When you understand the whole picture, that's where the real learning happens. That's where transformation begins.

WHY THE RICH?

People love a good story. Sports fans thrive when the underdog takes out their most hated rival. We cheer for the person who makes an incredible comeback against all odds. We stand and take notice when the overlooked, the downtrodden, and the never-coulds manage to succeed when almost everyone else counted them as good as done.

As a society, we also tend to love the *great fall.* We relish the stories of those who "have" suddenly finding themselves in the more crowded space of the "have-nots."

Many people feel disdain for those with money, as if they should finally suffer like we have for years. There's a belief that the rich didn't have to earn their money, that they must have inherited it. Or maybe they just got lucky. So when the rich lose, some people snicker. Some get giddy. Just the thought of those with wealth being humbled and maybe even humiliated can conjure up feelings of amusement, gratification, and a sense of satisfaction instead of empathy. Part of it is human nature, but part of it may stem from this idea that *the rich have some secret playbook or they've enjoyed certain advantages not available to the rest of us*.

As far as advantage is concerned, some certainly do, but I will tell you the majority earn their wealth. *And they have the same volatile relationship with money as the rest of us.* They can be just as inept at handling it as you or anyone else. Sure, the rich have better access to lawyers and legal loopholes, investment brokers and financial opportunities, but even those won't save them when they go too far and make too many mistakes.

While the majority of Americans are living paycheck to paycheck, the rich can just as easily be doing the same and find themselves teetering along the edge of bankruptcy, or worse. Yes, the rich lose. The rich go broke. And it's happening more frequently. Contrary to politically expedient talking points, while some of the poor may be getting poorer, many of the "rich" are getting poorer, too.

The rich in these stories are not much different than you and me. They made similar mistakes, albeit in a more grandiose fashion. The only difference is that they *had* wealth, and maybe even some degree of power, and lost it. The size of the loss is what makes these stories so powerful and useful. But the lesson is the same.

The cause of failure might be excessive greed or taking too great a financial risk that led to ruin. It may be poor planning or a lack of financial awareness, trying to portray an image or perhaps trying to take care of too many family members or friends.

My driving purpose in writing this book is to highlight the mistakes so many people make and *why* it can (and often does) lead to financial loss, and devastation. Errors in judgment, placing unnecessary value on image, and even trusting the wrong ideas, people, or motives can pull the rug right out from under anyone, no matter how much money they have in savings and investments, or are expecting through a career.

Simple mistakes comes from simple decisions, even seemingly harmless ones, but even a slight crack – over time – can bring down the strongest walls, mightiest fortresses, and tallest mountains.

YOUR TURN

It's time to dive into the *Guidebook* activities now. Let's start with Activity #1, which is to take the *FREE* personal assessment available at www.johnmacgregor.net.

Review the introduction to this free personal assessment in the guidebook. I highly encourage you to do this activity because it will lay a foundation essential to growth and eventual lasting change (and financial peace).

CHAPTER 3

Grandparents, Minnesota, and Lasagna

In order to understand where I'm coming from and how my views have been shaped through experience, it would be best for you to meet my grandparents.

Don and Julia MacGregor were not all that atypical of their era, although in my mind they were two of the most amazing people one could ever meet. They were a hard-working couple who survived the Great Depression. Because of that experience, they developed some keen and powerful lessons they carried for the rest of their lives.

These were lessons they passed on to their three children and, thankfully, their grandchildren. I was fortunate to be one of those who witnessed those lessons up close and in person.

When I was in the fourth grade, I made my first of many trips to Minnesota to spend the summer with my grandparents. They had five gorgeous acres on a lake they had named Loch Gregor to honor their Scottish ancestry. The property required never-ending upkeep to maintain its beauty. I would eventually spend every other summer there, earning $10 a day for my manual labor, which to me was a jackpot. That windfall would ultimately be my spending cash for the year.

Their property was exceptionally well-landscaped by their own hands. Flowers were meticulously planted in season. Gardens produced an abundance of fruits and vegetables. Massive birch, pine, and oak trees were everywhere, and apple trees were sprinkled throughout. Much of the property was adorned by a white wooden fence that seemed in constant need of fresh paint. I took on that project as well. More than once.

I cherished my summers in Minnesota. I loved spending time with my grandparents and being able to see other relatives. Frankly, I would have done the work for free. My grandparents were simply amazing people and I was blessed to be in their presence.

Every morning got off to an early start. At 6:45, Grandpa would yell downstairs, "Wake up, pumpkin head, it's daylight in the swamp!"

Bleary eyed, I'd make my way upstairs to a warm breakfast my grandmother prepared and I was expected to be there on time. By 7:30, the meal was over and I was out of the house to rake or mow or paint or weed (and weed some more) or do whatever tasks were set for me that day. Mornings were always dark, damp, and somewhat cold in Minnesota.

No matter how well I thought I had raked or weeded, Grandpa always found something I missed. He instilled in me the value of doing good work. You could rake a pile of leaves or weed the lakeshore for hours and be absolutely certain you got everything, but he always instructed me to keep going.

He was a perfectionist. Having graduated number one in his class from the Virginia Military Institute with a degree in Chemical Engineering, he had moved on to the Wharton School of Finance. He even turned down a full scholarship to MIT, despite the fact they'd waived his examination requirements. He served three years overseas in WWII and was part of the brutal Battle of Anzio. He was the third American to land on foreign soil in WWII.

My grandmother was an amazing person, too. She was talented in many things. Her fingers graced the ivories like a concert pianist until her final days. She raised three children during difficult times – much of it on her own while Grandpa Don was off fighting in Europe for those three years during WWII. The sacrifices they made for their family and their country were immeasurable, and millions of others did the same.

The work on the farm never ended. Today, we think of mowing the grass as an inconvenience, or we'll pay someone $50 to stop by once a week and spend 30 minutes rolling a machine over it and barely think twice. In those days at the farm, the tractor was slow, but it was far better than a sickle.

I swore I could actually see the grass growing right in front of my eyes, and the weeds … well, they sprouted like you-know-what. Just when I thought I was getting on top of things, I'd turn around and there, behind me, I'd see that the field I had tended to the previous day was already showing signs of new growth.

Sundays were supposed to be our day of rest, as mandated by Grandma. But after church, Grandpa and I would sneak out and find some kind of work, making sure we didn't use any equipment that made noise so as to not get caught.

Every day we'd wrap up the morning at 11, and by 11:30 we were headed downtown to the St. Paul Athletic Club. It was surreal knowing my own father had been a shoeshine boy, locker room attendant, and swim instructor at the same club back in the mid '40s. While Grandpa went off to a private room to have lunch and play cards with his buddies, I'd head to the gym to prepare for the upcoming football season.

There were more than a few times I was invited to play some hands of gin rummy (for money) with the gentlemen before heading back to the homestead, and you'd better believe I never turned down an opportunity. Once we got home, though, it was back to work for a few more hours.

And that's how life was on the farm in Minnesota. While I learned the incredible lessons of hard, rewarding work, there were some more powerful lessons slipping through the layers of my young mind.

Every afternoon, without exception, Grandpa would pull out this massive ledger and flip through dozens of pages filled with red, black, and blue ink. In that book, he would jot down every expense. It didn't matter if it was for the electric bill, a bottle of milk, or their tithing; *everything* was noted. He was as meticulous with his money as he was his yardwork.

One afternoon I happened to be inside as a thunderstorm rolled across the region. I was watching my grandfather from the entryway of the house, and my grandmother was watching me to make sure I didn't step on the carpet! Grandpa knew I was there, but his accounting work was top priority at that time. I asked what he was doing, but he continued poring through his financial records. It was the end of the month and he was conducting a regular audit of their financial situation and reconciling everything to make sure he knew precisely where they were financially. He ran the family finances like a chief financial officer would a company.

My grandparents monitored and recorded every penny. They could both tell you where each cent was invested, how it was doing, and what they had in their bank account. They were meticulous. None of this was done in a vacuum, either; my grandmother was privy to everything.

Nothing was left to chance. In fact, rarely did they let the gas tank in their car drop below three-quarters because "you never know what could happen." Those painful memories of the Great Depression would never leave them. They felt the need to always be prepared for the worst.

One morning, after breakfast was cleared, before I managed to drag myself outside for another day of physical labor, I saw Grandma cleaning out the toaster tray. She drew it out with great care. I expected her to dump the crumbs into the sink, but she carefully dropped them into a plastic bag in the midst of other, older crumbs. She spotted my curious expression and said with a confidence I'll never forget, "Never waste a crumb." To me, they were just crumbs, something to be discarded and something that would attract ants if they weren't. To her, they still had a use to cook with or sprinkle on a salad. They still held value!

My grandparents didn't even own a garbage disposal. They didn't need one, as no food was ever thrown away. The mere notion would make their heads shake in confusion. Whatever wasn't finished at a meal was carefully saved and consumed later.

If you don't know what it was like for millions of people living through the Great Depression, imagine wondering if you would eat (forget about *what* you'd eat, but **whether** you would). Imagine relying on your children to bring in extra money so you could buy food and scrape out one more day. That was their life. My dad often talks about those times not with regret or animosity but with a sense of pride for what his parents were able to do and who they became.

Despite the rigors of life back then, **happiness, pride,** and **grateful** are words that seemed to weave throughout every story they told. Yes, it was tough, and they had to fight for so much of what we take for granted today, but they always felt blessed to have a roof over their heads and food on the table.

Grandpa and Grandma knew what it was like to go without, as did so many others. It's one of the key reasons people of that generation were so intent on saving, saving, saving. They knew what survival was really like. They cherished life but did so modestly.

Many years ago, my grandparents were interviewed for an article asking what it was like to live through the Great Depression in Duluth, Minnesota, one of the coldest spots in the United States. Here's what they said:

__Donald (Grandpa):__ During the Depression, Duluth was very hard hit. A lot of people lost everything. You had to kind of live by your

wits during those times. Business was so poor, they called me in and said, "Business is awful, your salary is now $100 a month plus commissions." And there weren't any commissions. Meantime, I had a wife and three children. And I owed the bank $7,000, which was $35 a month of interest at 6 percent. So that left me $65. I was in the National Guard, so I had an additional income of $55 a month, which included drill pay once a week and summer camp for two weeks. That left me with $120 per month. And my wife Julie was teaching piano and had a little income as well ($1.25 per lesson).

But every month I went over to this bank and paid them the $35 interest. Finally, the clerk said, "Mr. MacGregor, the president of the bank wants to see you." He said to me, "Where's our money?" I said, "I just left it with the clerk." "That's the interest. We want our *money." So I proceeded to give him a hard luck story. And I said, "This isn't the worst loan you've got. I'm not going bankrupt, and if it takes me the rest of my life, I'm going to pay it off." "Well that's your tough luck," he said to me. He was a tough cookie ... Well, it was a tough period and I developed stomach trouble, which meant medical bills to pay.*

Julie (Grandma): Of course, I had to skimp too, along the way. We had a garden which we depended on a great deal. We canned vegetables and picked raspberries, apples and so forth. And I'd buy a pot roast, for instance, and it would have to last all week, in one form or another. The children had to help, too, in that garden. We had no vacation, of course. The boys had paper routes where we lived, they had to walk long distances in the snow. Even Judy, our daughter, peddled raspberries down the block to our neighbors. Shopping meant planning meals for a whole week and buying only the absolute necessities. But I'll tell you, even so, I think we were as happy then, as I look back, as we've ever been.

NEVER OWNED A CREDIT CARD

Despite the fact that they were eventually able to overcome these financial challenges, those experiences led my grandparents to save everything throughout their entire lives. My grandmother would clip every coupon she could and on occasion I'd ride with her into town, where she'd go from one store to the next, spending hours doing what can be finished in mere minutes today. She *had* to get the best deals. On everything. Regardless of what it took to do so.

I recall one day we drove a few extra miles to a store to buy a six-pack of Kleenex boxes because of a coupon she had clipped from the newspaper. The fact that they were a clearance item featuring a Star Wars theme didn't matter. It was the price that mattered most and the extra drive it took to get them was inconsequential. I can remember thinking, *Where are you going to put these?* It was a question I never dared ask.

One of the most upsetting yet strangely rewarding experiences of my life happened during my second summer with them.

My grandmother wanted me to meet a great-aunt of mine, so the three of us went to lunch. Lunch! Eating out wasn't something they did often.

As we sat in this coffee shop in a downtown shopping mall, the waiter asked what I wanted. I love Italian food, so I ordered the lasagna. Never in my wildest imagination did I foresee the consequences of that order. To this day, it still haunts me when I hear the word "lasagna;" I cannot help but think of this memory.

"Are you sure that's what you want?" my grandmother asked.

I nodded.

"Is that *really* what you want?" she prodded again.

"Yes, please." I was sure.

I couldn't tell you a single thing about the lasagna. Not the salad that came first, not the sauce, not the meat. Nothing. The food wasn't memorable in the least.

Well, very quickly I found out the reason for her questions.

"Was your lasagna good?" she asked me when the meal was finished.

"Yeah."

"I would certainly hope so." She sniffed. "Your great-aunt and I ordered soup and sandwich for $5. Your lasagna was $7."

At first I was stunned. I didn't know what to say. I quickly realized that we had a problem. Scratch that. *I* had a problem.

This shaming went on for some time. It was as though I had ordered filet mignon and lobster. I was stunned. After all, we were at a no-frills restaurant in a mall and I hadn't bothered to look at the price of anything; I'd merely done as I was told: order what I wanted. To put it mildly, it was a long and uncomfortable ride home.

This was the first – and thankfully the last – time she ever scolded me, and boy did I feel terrible. I sulked and moped and when I got home I spent hours in my room wondering what to do next. I finally took some of the money I had earned and left the entire cost of the lasagna on her nightstand. I was upset. I was frustrated. I was embarrassed. That act was my way of saying sorry.

My grandfather did his best to calm the stormy seas, but I would, from that moment on, always know I had let her down. I probably let him down as well, which made the situation even worse. In time, the frustration I'd felt toward her became directed at myself, and to this day, when I recall that moment, I still feel the stress. I feel the shame. I feel the hurt. It still haunts me when I hear the word "lasagna."

I realized in time that, for her, the scolding was simply a reflection of how she had been raised, how she'd learned to survive in a time I hope we never have to experience again. She never wanted to hurt me or make me feel bad. Her reaction was her survival response, and in a strict yet loving way, she was trying to teach me a lesson and protect me for my future.

Please don't get the wrong impression; my grandparents were extremely generous people. Despite the financial squeeze they had to endure, they were always willing to give. Their generosity to the church, local causes, their respective alma maters, and the family was something I look at in amazement, even to this day. It was their generosity that has motivated me to do the same in my life.

Years after the economy recovered and they managed to get on solid financial footing, their desire to save never ended. When they would visit us in Hawaii, my grandmother and my mom would go shopping for clothes. At my grandmother's insistence, their shopping spree would begin at thrift stores.

My grandparents were never rich (my grandfather never made more than $25,000 a year as a Vice President of the First National Bank of St. Paul), but over time they grew their wealth slowly and methodically and they were able to amass a commendable net worth, even by today's standards.

Their first big purchase, using borrowed money, was a large piece of land surrounding a beautiful lake. They kept one parcel for themselves to build their home and sold the rest. Each lot sold for approximately $6,000. From the proceeds of those sales, after paying off the loan, they put that money in stodgy blue-chip stocks and collected the dividends. They held these stocks – in good financial times and bad – and the stocks gained tremendous value through the years. At Christmas, my grandparents would gift each grandchild shares of stock for our future nest eggs. Although some of my stocks were used to pay for college, I still own a significant number of shares today.

They traveled every year for weeks at a time in their 60s and 70s – trips to visit us in Hawaii, cruises all over the world, and travels to one of their favorite spots, Tanque Verde Ranch, an all-inclusive guest ranch in Tucson, Arizona. As our family spread across the country, every five years or so they would cover all the costs for the 20-plus family members to get together for a week-long reunion in places such as Mexico, Santa Barbara, and Arizona.

Through wise investments and shrewd spending habits and no credit card debt, they were able to enjoy an amazing retirement and still have a lot left over to pass on to future generations. They lived happily in retirement, traveled, and enjoyed their time together. To them, money didn't buy happiness; time together did. Money was a tool to fulfill their purpose, not to impress others. Nothing more.

Growing up during tough times like they did, they learned to respect money in ways few can relate to in our modern society. Theirs is an inspirational story, and my grandfather and grandmother taught me the value of hard, honest work and the true value of money.

YOUR TURN
Turn to the guidebook and Activity #2. It shouldn't take you too long, but it's good to get this done now. Later, you may reflect back on your answers for this activity and see a change in your attitude or focus.

CHAPTER 4

The Trap

Despite all the many reasons people – rich and poor – struggle financially, I've found an underlying commonality. As a result, I developed a principle that encompasses them all: ***The B.E.A.R. Trap.***

The B.E.A.R. Trap is an apt metaphor for the situation so many people find them-selves in. Whether they were going along seemingly fine with every-thing in order, or they were struggling day to day to keep their head above water, B.E.A.R. is an acronym that gets to the core of *why* so many people, rich and poor, make decisions that lead to personal and financial destruction:

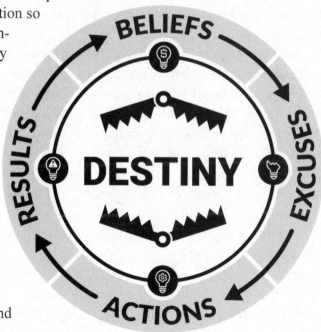

= YOUR DESTINY

B.E.A.R. is an insidious chain reaction that has powerful and consequential effects that ultimately lead to one's destiny. It is here where your harmful *Beliefs* around money turn into damaging *Excuses*, which lead to destructive *Actions*, which in turn end in painful *Results*. This ripple effect you endure every single day is, in essence, your ***DESTINY***.

When we're unhappy with the results of something, it isn't enough to understand what actions we should have taken. For lasting change, we need to understand why we started down that destructive path in the first place or took that left turn when we should have kept going straight. By simply focusing on the *What* versus the *Why* we are far more likely to repeat these mistakes over and over.

So much of our financial struggle is tied to our mental programming. We far too often try external solutions when, in fact, the problem is internal. The wonderful news is that there's nothing physically wrong with you and that your problems may be a lot easier to fix than you've been led to believe.

BEGINNING WITH BELIEFS

Let's start with the first and most critical stage of B.E.A.R. – the *B* stands for *Belief.*

Beliefs work in your subconscious, essentially determining what you do, say, think, and ultimately become whether you realize it or not.

Think about this: your subconscious mind can process over forty million nerve impulses every second. It's the most powerful processor in the world and it exists within each of us. These nerve impulses play the same tape over and over again like a broken record.

Our entire lives are built on the foundation of our beliefs. In fact, research suggests that 95% of our experiences and decisions come from our beliefs. In other words, 95% of who we are in the world lies in our subconscious, or the term I prefer, our *unconscious.*

Bruce H. Lipton, Ph.D., is an internationally recognized leader in bridging science and personal success. "So by definition," he says, "your life is a printout of your unconscious programming. What is troubling is that you play these programs 95% of the time and you don't see them, so that means at least 95% of the time you are sabotaging yourself and you don't see it. Therefore you never understood why things in your life were not working."

Think of your subconscious like a computer program running repeatedly. A majority of these programs in your subconscious mind were downloaded and embedded into the code of your life by the time you were seven years old. These programs were based on what you observed as a child; essentially your life becomes an expression of other people's behavior. These experiences shape us into who we become as individuals. And research has revealed that 70% of those programs are negative and disempowering.

As we grow, become educated, and begin experiencing the world, gaining more and more independence, our beliefs may shift and adjust. But by the time we're 18 our beliefs are hard wired in our brains.

So, if 95% of our life is running in our unconscious without our awareness – completely on autopilot dictating what we think, believe, and ultimately become – that means we're only aware of 5% of our conscious activity.

And what are these programs running in the background and controlling 95% of your life?

These programs are made up of your *beliefs* and most people have harmful beliefs that are not in line with their wishes and desires.

I've discovered that a primary reason people struggle financially is they have harmful beliefs involving money and these beliefs are the root cause of their stress and are literally killing them.

CLINGING TO OLD BELIEFS

Our beliefs are our framework for how we think and act. But our beliefs aren't reality; they're our opinions of what we believe to be true. These opinions closely determine our actions.

And yet we rarely test them, even as circumstances change.

Throughout your childhood, teenage years, and young adult life, you develop an overall behavior pattern called your **Winning Strategy.** This strategy allows you to survive and thrive in your environment at that time.

Now, you may be wondering how this can be your winning strategy when you're barely surviving in your current financial situation. Well, think of it this way: when you were a youngster, your early belief structures were reinforced when they led to feelings of joy, peace, success, harmony, and acceptance by others. They worked for you or for others in your familiar circle. These beliefs eventually became your playbook, your operating manual that showed you how to navigate through life. As you used these strategies, they continued to work for you.

One example of this is that many children, after watching the spending habits of their parents, have grown up believing that *money grows on trees.* This idea has been a root cause for so many people especially when they are suddenly faced with the need to provide for themselves yet still have an insatiable appetite for more stuff.

These beliefs became hard wired in your brain.

Every new thing that comes into your life – good, bad, or indifferent – is filtered through this unconscious belief system that was constructed based on a "winning strategy" that's now causing you harm and disempowerment. This is how most people live their lives. What's worse is that they're totally unaware that this is the case. Most people don't want to confront the truth because they fear destroying their illusions.

It's highly likely you're reading this book because your current belief structure worked in the past but no longer does in your adult decision-making environment. In other words, your belief systems aren't helping you when it matters most!

Even when you're confronted with a new reality or truth, ingrained beliefs can be incredibly stubborn. Maybe that new career you began 10 years ago hasn't led to the promotions you expected. Or you haven't been the salesperson you expected and the results and commissions are far from where you thought they'd be. Perhaps you started a new business with huge hopes and expectations, only to realize it has become a major money pit. Perhaps you simply gave up trying because you were convinced that things will never work out for you.

Some people become so rooted in their beliefs (even though there may not be any actual evidence to support them) that they refuse to listen to facts that counter them.

EXPLORING HARMFUL BELIEFS

My friend Gary van Warmerdam, a thought leader in the science of cognitive transformation and founder of Pathway to Happiness, provides a perfect analogy to describe how old beliefs can sabotage us. He says:

Think about it like this – our bodies are like big computers, and beliefs are like the software operating system of that computer. Many of the beliefs that you have are the equivalent of viruses, actually causing harmful, self-destructive behaviors. The reason things aren't working for you right now is because you have a set of false beliefs that are dictating your sabotaging behavior. Those beliefs are the

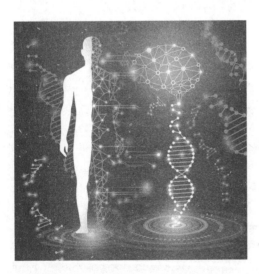

software wired through the neural pathways of your brain. Your operating system – i.e., your "software" – is not running properly and is likely out of date. What you learned to believe about yourself and money at age 5, 10, and 15 is still running in the background. There's nothing wrong with you physically; we simply need to run an anti-virus program to get those neural structures firing in a different and more effective manner. The way the world and yourself appear to you – i.e., what is on your computer monitor – is a direct result of these beliefs. To change that appearance, you cannot simply take whiteout and cover up those flaws on the computer screen. What you need to do is address the operating system and its software.

So let me ask you: is it possible that you have a virus that is preventing you from having a good relationship with money? What are your thoughts as you ponder the sources of your current financial situation? What might some of these viruses look like?

- Frustration about your state of progress
- Procrastination
- Fear of failing
- Judgment, envy, or resentment of others' success
- The need for "stuff" you must have but know you can't afford
- Criticism of others' failures
- Self-criticism over decisions you made
- Feelings of inadequacy, insecurity, or low self-worth associated with money
- Thoughts of how great your life would be if you had more money
- The need for an image in order to impress others
- Excessive excitement over high-risk investment opportunities
- Fear of investment opportunities
- Fear of missing out on the next boom opportunity

Remember, beliefs shape your financial decisions. For example, if you believe this new career you've set out on is going to give you the opportunity to make a fortune, maybe you don't wait to begin purchasing the material possessions you've always dreamed about.

You believe the money's going to roll in, so you buy the big house, the fancy car, or the huge entertainment system. Maybe you even take an expensive vacation or two to exotic destinations.

When things don't pan out, do you change your spending habits? Do you downsize that house you're spending 60% of your post-tax income on? Or do you make excuses?

"I need to look the part."

"This makes me happy."

"Will my family and friends think of me as a failure if I downsize?"

Beliefs are often used as justification to avoid what you need to do –

29

what you *know* you need to do. Beliefs are used as an excuse for why you are who you are.

In a way, beliefs give you an "out."

In the work I do with people, I purposely spend considerable time upfront uncovering a person's harmful beliefs and how they are literally driving themselves into financial submission. It's these harmful beliefs that are the genesis behind a person's unhealthy relationship with money and, sadly, the cause that perpetuates this cycle of pain so many are unnecessarily enduring every single day. The financial community has completely ignored this vital component.

The graph above illustrates how people can be perpetually stuck in the circular B.E.A.R. Trap if they don't recognize their harmful beliefs and acknowledge that it's here where their problems lie.

Once you make that shift to New Beliefs, you're in a far better position to avoid those Recurring Excuses, so you can now take Positive Actions that *will* ultimately lead to Prosperous Results.

Here's a list of some of the most common harmful beliefs around money I've heard over the years. Do any of these sound familiar?

- *"I'll never be good with money"*
- *"I'm not good with numbers"*
- *"The system is rigged and unfair"*
- *"I didn't come from money"*
- *"Money is the root of all evil"*
- *"There's more to life than money"*
- *"With two jobs and a family, I don't have time to take care of my finances"*
- *"Someone else will take care of me/us."*
- *"Money causes stress in my life"*
- *"Wealthy people are greedy and evil"*
- *"I'm stuck in a rut"*
- *"What's spending just a little more money going to hurt?"*
- *"I don't like to take risks"*
- *"I have to have this new _____"*
- *"It's only $100 per month on my credit card"*
- *"I can worry about the future later"*
- *"It's vital I send my kids to college"*

You make your beliefs and then your beliefs make you.

In a way, beliefs have become people's identity and this identity has become their unhealthy sanctuary.

Please take a moment and think about these harmful beliefs listed above, or perhaps others that come to mind, and how they may apply to you. Refer to the graph and how "the shift" could, in fact, radically change your life and circumstances.

> **In a way, beliefs have become people's identity and this identity has become their unhealthy sanctuary.**

EXCUSES, ACTIONS, AND RESULTS

Stage 2 of the B.E.A.R. Trap is *E*: *Excuses*.

Often I hear, "I don't have time ... I'll take care of it later, next month, next year ..." Such *excuses* are rooted in a harmful underlying belief that time and time again has wreaked havoc on people's financial situations; the belief that nothing bad can happen.

Excuses create a cycle that return you back to your beliefs, no matter how flawed or inaccurate they are, and you rely on your built-in excuses (*based* on your beliefs) to keep you rooted in the same bad habits.

Given enough time – and enough excuses – you're led to unhealthy and detrimental outcomes.

You feel stressed and frustrated, so you take an unplanned day off from work, drop several grand on a second or third vacation to a tropical destination, or upgrade your flat screen television even though you can't really afford it. You routinely swipe your credit card to soothe the pain, even though you'll struggle to pay it off for months or years.

You rack up more credit card debt and treat yourself to pricey new gadgets or new clothes. You stop by for some gas on the way to work, see the Mega Millions jackpot has reached $1.53 billion, and decide to grab $20 worth of tickets. Even though you don't win that time, you're convinced it could happen on the next Friday or Saturday jackpot drawing, so you get into another bad habit.

You start tripping into a number of bad habits and vices in an effort to quell the pain you feel because of your poor set of beliefs.

With enough time, all those excuses will lead to bad decisions. These bad decisions are your *A*, *Actions* (Step 3).

These include actually **buying** those material things you don't actually need and can't honestly afford (without putting yourself in a deeper financial hole).

Your actions could be avoiding your spouse, spending more time at work or at the local bar before heading home because you don't want to confront the questions he or she will have about your finances.

Doing nothing – in other words *inaction* – is no different than an *action*. Not doing something is still making a decision. A choice.

You start to develop a pattern of lies to cover up the mistakes you've made. Maybe you gloss over your work life, say "everything's going great" when you know tomorrow might leave you without a job.

The more you get away with the lies, the easier they become and eventually you discover that even though there's no point in telling your spouse or friend or boss or coworker a lie, you do it, because it's "easier" at the moment.

The stress mounts, compounding the struggle you have in your mind. You take on more bad habits in an effort to cover the pain and worry and stress and anxiety you're feeling and it's not helping. It's only driving you deeper into a dark place you don't want to be.

These *actions* will ultimately produce *R, Results* (Step 4) that you didn't expect and certainly don't want.

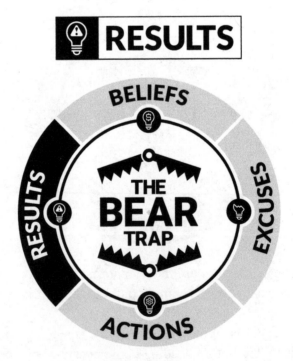

The results can be a loss of your job, a loss of income, a loss of savings, broken marriages, broken homes, poor health, and bankruptcy. You get into this pattern where you base your excuses on beliefs that were never rooted in truth. You use those excuses to justify the actions that follow. Those actions, over time, become more addictions, more bad decisions, and while you begin spinning your wheels, the results start pouring in.

You may not see just how messed up everything is until the mountain comes crumbling down on top of you. You build your entire life on a foundation of sand, assuming no storm is going to strike.

When it does, you're taken by surprise.

QUESTIONING BELIEFS

The B.E.A.R. Trap does not discriminate. It doesn't care about the color of your skin, your gender, your education, where you were born, your culture, your political beliefs and ideologies, your religion, or anything else. While the uber-rich are much less susceptible to detrimental consequences from bad decisions, there are many instances where these men and women have lost everything, too. It's likely you've heard the stories of famous people who were on top of the world, only to see their lives shattered.

José Canseco, Stephen Baldwin, Patricia Kluge, Leon Spinks, Mike Tyson, Larry King, MC Hammer, Willie Nelson, Gary Busey, Nicholas Cage, Henry Ford, Halsey Minor, Wesley Snipes, Alberto Vilar, JC Penney, Debbie Reynolds, Jordan Belfort, Sean Quinn, Walt Disney, P.T. Barnum, Mark Twain, and the list goes on. Some of the people on this list were once *billionaires* who declared bankruptcy and *still owed* more debt than they could pay.

When you drill down to the core of every one of these once wealthy and powerful people, you will discover that the key reason they lost everything was due to a harmful belief system. Period

The purpose of this book isn't just to tell you what happened; this book digs down to the *"why"* they lost everything.

It's happened over and over to men and women who could have enjoyed the best of wealth for the rest of their lives had they been aware of the B.E.A.R. Trap. While a few managed to leverage their celebrity status, business reputation, and other assets to regain some of their past "glory," most of the time these stories lead to long, drawn out struggles to regain footing.

If you're rooted in your beliefs and refuse to acknowledge that something about them could be wrong, you're walking through the woods completely oblivious to the pitfalls, cliff faces, and bear traps that surround you.

An age-old adage states, "Your beliefs become your thoughts. Your thoughts become your words. Your words become your actions. Your actions become your habits. Your habits become your values. Your values become your destiny."

> **"Your beliefs become your thoughts. Your thoughts become your words. Your words become your actions. Your actions become your habits. Your habits become your values. Your values become your destiny."**

In other words, *Your beliefs become your destiny.*

Everything starts with your beliefs. A flawed belief system, no matter the reason for the flaw (experience, childhood, abuse, failed relationships or marriages, social media, witnessing violence and screaming between your parents, or anything else), is going to shape every other aspect of your life.

You first need to recognize and acknowledge your beliefs and determine how and why you have them. There may be some beliefs you'll hold onto for the rest of your life, and that's fine. However, if those beliefs put you in harm's way, how could they possibly be beneficial?

You may be thinking I'm talking about your religious beliefs, your political beliefs, your sports beliefs, and so on. I'm not … although this lesson can apply to all aspects of your life. This book is specifically focused on the beliefs that shape your financial habits.

I want to get you out of that B.E.A.R. Trap, make the shift, or better yet, avoid it altogether.

YOUR TURN

Now it's your turn. Activity #3 in the guidebook is the most labor intensive for you, but it's crucial to the learning process.

No matter how long it takes, I implore you to be diligent and patient with it. Close the door, turn off the music, and treat this activity like you would a major assignment at work, something that *has* to be done – and done well.

The more effort you put in now, the more dividends you'll earn later on.

I promise.

CHAPTER 5

How Bad Is It?

Look around and you may assume that life in the United States is pretty darn good. Children head off to colleges in droves. People drive $35,000 cars, $55,000 SUVs and souped-up pickup trucks, and $100,000 luxury sedans without a second thought.

In certain parts of the country, the average new home construction involves houses *starting* at $600,000. Rent in New England, Southern California, and many other highly populated regions across the country could run well over $5,000 a month or more, and that's just for a basic three-bedroom house with very little lawn.

To somebody coming into this country for the first time who had no idea what America was, is, or will be, it would appear as though we're super rich. And compared to the rest of the world, we are (though much of that wealth, in terms of cars and houses and material items, is nothing more than illusion, bought and paid for in debt).

Make no mistake about it: no matter what your financial situation is, even if you or somebody you know is living right around the poverty line, they are wealthier than the majority of the world.

We have smartphones that may cost over $120 a month (just to keep them active, forget the $1,000 price tag). We have cable and internet at home that could rack up at least $160 to $220, on average, every single month. A quick fast food meal at McDonald's or In-N-Out Burger is going to set you back almost $10, and that's just for you, by yourself. A quick dinner out on a date with your spouse, somebody you're trying to impress, or even a colleague or business associate can easily jump to $50 or $75 for just two people, after tip (and that's without drinks factored in). The average American is heading out to eat at a restaurant or fast food establishment, on average, 15 to 20 times every single month.

So much money is spent on things *we don't need,* but what's even more troubling is that the vast majority of these nonessential items have somehow transformed into necessities in our minds.

But if you have all this money, why can't you spend it?

There's your belief system at work.

Why can't you? You can. I'm not telling you that you can't. What I'm getting at here is that a belief system we have built up in this country – based on inadequate financial education early in life and multibillion-dollar marketing campaigns – has created an idea, a distortion of what money truly is, what it represents, and how it affects each one of us.

We want the new 65-inch U-screen TV because we "deserve it." Forget the fact it's going to set us back $2,500 after paying the principal and interest. Or we get tired of the 5-year-old car and see an "incredible" offer on a new vehicle, so we drop ourselves $40,000 deeper into debt with a $400-per-month payment for six years.

> **We're thinking little of the consequences our actions will have on our future. Our belief system has been built around *immediate* reward.**

We're thinking little of the consequences our actions will have on our future. Our belief system has been built around *immediate* reward.

LIVING PAYCHECK TO PAYCHECK

Let me remind you of a sobering statistic.

78% of people in the United States are living paycheck to paycheck. 78%!

What does that mean? It means that nearly 8 out of every 10 Americans are waiting for their next paycheck to cover basic living expenses, including their electric bill, phone bill, mortgage, rent, and credit card bills – or even to fill up their gas tank. As most people are working steady, full-time jobs, they understand exactly how much they're going to get, after taxes, after their 401(k) contributions, and after any other expenses, including medical or dental coverage, every single paycheck.

Most Americans receive a paycheck every two weeks. Some get it weekly, some monthly, and some at a different interval.

Because they know exactly what's going to be deposited into their checking or savings account every two weeks, for example, they know exactly how much they can spend.

However, we also have credit. Credit cards, home equity loans, payday loans, title loans (targeting lower income people most), and a host of other opportunities allow people to get a false sense of security that they can buy something they want *now* and pay it off in the next 12 to 60 months and everything's going to be fine. Many consider credit to be "free money" or "instant cash."

What happens if an emergency arises?

Approximately 26% of American adults have absolutely zero savings. 36% haven't even started putting money away for retirement, and we're not just talking about 20-somethings but people in their 30s, 40s, and 50s.

The average American bank savings account has about $3,400 in it. Before you get all excited, realize that "average" accounts for *everyone*, even those who may have $0 on their balance sheet.

The personal savings rate for U.S. citizens in 2012 was 10.5%. That's not a great number, but it wasn't terrible. In 2014, the rate plummeted to 4.4% (creditdonkey.com).

As far as that potential emergency situation that might arise, 64% of Americans could not come up with $400 today for an emergency.

> **64% of Americans could not come up with $400 today for an emergency**

They would have to beg, borrow, or do something else to quickly earn money if their car broke down, the furnace busted, or they faced a serious medical emergency. They would, in effect, be financially devastated from an emergency that might cost them a few thousand dollars.

THE STUDENT LOAN DEBACLE

Even in light of this serious personal debt and savings problem, perhaps the biggest issue facing a growing number of Americans today is student loan debt.

Currently, the total student loan debt in the U.S. sits at $1.5 *trillion*. It's the biggest source of personal debt next to mortgages.

This crisis has the potential to utterly destroy the prospects of an entire generation … make that *several* generations! If you've ever wondered why growing voices of young adults support socialistic ideas, this is one of the prime reasons. Who wants to be saddled with staggering debts that'll take decades to pay off just for a college degree?

Many students taking out loans for college don't even graduate. It's taking longer and longer for our young adults to graduate. Just 6 in 10 college students graduate in six years.

Since 1978, the cost of college has risen over 1,000%. College tuition has increased twice as fast as medical care costs. 1 in 3 are delinquent on their loans. 1 in 5 students are in default.

While young generations have become convinced that the *only* way to get ahead in life is with a college degree (a fallacy), universities have capitalized on the influx of guaranteed cash through these student loan programs and have jacked up tuition fees by a staggering degree, far outpacing inflation.

Many students find themselves in jobs where the imbalance between the cost to earn that degree and what they make in salary means they'll likely *never* pay off the loan. Student loan debt is growing faster than wages are increasing.

Over two million Americans now owe more than $100,000 in student loans. If you start life off that deep in the hole, it could take you 20 to 30 years *just to pay it off!*

It's out of control and only getting worse.

You have to ask yourself the question: Is college really worth it?

PENSION PROBLEMS

There are tens of millions of people basing their retirement on a promised pension. Yet we are in the midst of a pension crisis. Social Security is on track to be bankrupt in 2034 (that's just over 14 years from the printing of this book), and many cities and states are in so much debt they couldn't possibly honor the financial promises they made to their state level employees to cover pensions in 10, 20, or 30 years.

According to the Social Security Administration, 62% of retired workers rely on Social Security payments for at least half their monthly income. 34% of retirees rely on Social Security payments for 90-100% of their total income.

It wasn't designed for that. It was intended as a supplemental support system, but during the past few decades it's transformed into a nest egg all by itself.

Why is no one sounding the alarm bells?

A few people are. But most just aren't listening.

Why?

Because of their *beliefs.*

They believe everything that they have right now is how things will be tomorrow, next year, in 10 years, or when they retire. They believe the promises made to them (especially by the government or a union) will be honored.

They can't and don't want to even *think* there's a possibility they will reach retirement and the pension fund will be empty. But it's happened.

Pension debt is not a new story – in fact, most of the country's public pensions are significantly underfunded (state and local pensions across the U.S. have an estimated $5 trillion less than needed to cover promised benefits).

It happened with businesses as well, many of which are no longer around. It happened with Worldcom. It happened with Enron. It happened with United Airlines. It has happened in Greece and other countries. It is happening in Venezuela, Spain, Portugal, Argentina and Italy just to name a few. It is happening in many other places around the world. And it's now starting to happen is various states across the U.S. – namely California, Michigan, Connecticut, Illinois, Kentucky, New Jersey, my home state of Hawaii, and yes, even in New York which is considered the world's leading financial center.

Recently, the U.S. Treasury Department permitted Ironworkers Local 17 in Ohio to cut retiree benefits by as much as 50%. This ruling will now pit current ironworkers against retired workers in a vote to approve. If it's not approved, current workers stand to lose as much, if not more, than retirees. Sadly, some of these beneficiaries could lose everything.

This is just the tip of the iceberg as more and more stories are emerging of pension cuts across the country.

This is a major crisis taking shape across the country, and it's not getting better. Currently, there are over 67 multi-employer pension plans that cover about 1 million workers that have filed applications with the government to be classified as "critical and declining." That means these pensions could be cut in the same way as the Ironworkers Local 17 plan, if not more drastically.

As of this writing, four plans were denied requested cuts because the government ruled the cuts weren't *enough* to maintain the integrity of those pensions.

People have constantly been over-promised while the pensions have been underfunded, and just like the 78% of Americans living paycheck to paycheck, many of these pensions are one disaster away from complete meltdown.

It's frightening. And sobering.

It will happen again.

I'm not going to get into a political debate about which party has better ideas or which is more rooted in reality than another. This isn't about politics. It's too late for that. This is now about *personal responsibility*.

This is all about your mindset and how you move forward from here. In other words, this is about *your* beliefs and how your beliefs are going to directly affect your future, your finances, and probably even your family and relationships.

How about a sobering *new* story in the Wall Street Journal that came down the pipe July 25, 2019. The title of this article is: "The Plan to Save Truckers' and Miners' Pensions Is Running Out of Time." The subtitle: "House approves $48.5 billion package offering forgivable loans to the most troubled multiemployer pension funds."

I don't know about you, but I doubt I'd ever qualify for a "forgivable" loan from anyone, much less the government.

Today, as of this writing, General Electric, "GE," who just recently was one of the largest, most diversified, and most admired companies in the world, just announced they are freezing their pension plan for 20,000 employees. Today, they have one of the largest pension shortfalls in Corporate America. No one could have ever predicted this. It's absolutely stunning to have witnessed the demise of such a powerful and highly respected company.

Here are some sobering details:

- The pensions for 1.3 million truckers and miners are in jeopardy.
- Plans in the worst shape are short $100 *billion*.
- This House passed plan only bails out the most troubled and still doesn't give enough to save them.
- The government insurance program designed to backstop these pensions has warned it expects to run out of money by 2025.
- Out of the 10 million or so workers and retirees who participate in multiemployer plans, a significant percentage could end up receiving a fraction of promised benefits.
- Anticipating $12,870 a year for 30 years of service could actually be as little as $643 a year.

What's more, as the article notes, "The PBGC's projection of a $100 billion shortfall for the plans in the worst condition is based on a conservative return projection. But the plans themselves use higher rates that can lead to shortfalls if returns don't materialize as expected. Forcing the better-funded plans to use more-conservative rates – a possibility contemplated by lawmakers last year – would make the financial problems in multiemployer plans look even more widespread."[1]

SUFFERING STRESS

The result of all of this is devastating. Yet, sadly, for the most part it's being ignored.

Most people understand the impact stress can have on their lives. Financial situations, including bills, debts, and medical expenses, are the number one stressor for Americans (CBS)[2]. In other words, people stress about money more than they stress about anything else in life. It's not because they want to stress about these things but because financial stressors impact our lives so intimately and directly.

Why does this matter? Stress has a grave impact on health. It leads to a host of health issues, from anxiety to elevated blood pressure to an increased risk of heart attack and stroke. The longer stress endures, the greater the risk of:

- Insomnia
- Heart disease
- Obesity
- Asthma
- Diabetes
- Cirrhosis
- Headaches
- Depression
- Accelerated aging
- And more

All these health-related problems increase the amount of money we need to devote to medical care, which exacerbates our money problems and stress and, yes, health issues.

---

1   https://www.wsj.com/articles/the-plan-to-save-truckers-and-miners-pensions-is-running-out-of-time-11564053282

2   https://www.cbsnews.com/news/the-biggest-cause-of-stress-in-america-today/

More than 75% of all physician office visits are the direct result of stress-related ailments and complaints. Before you read on, let that simple statistic soak in for a minute.

Three quarters of *all* visits to a doctor's office have nothing to do with regular check-ups but are the direct and indirect result of stress-related illnesses, ailments, and complaints.

Unlike other stressors that are temporary, like fighting through traffic, a job interview, or that first date, financial

> **More than 75% of all physician office visits are the direct result of stress-related ailments and complaints**

stress wears on you daily. It is a constant never-ending source of stress and anxiety. It pounds on you day after day, night after night without remorse or relief.

A person who is constantly dealing with stress and anxiety because of financial pressure could face an even greater obstacle if they suddenly have a heart attack, are diagnosed with cancer, or face another monumental challenge in life. After all, how are they even going to think about paying for medical treatment, even if they have insurance? Most health insurance policies today have a minimum deductible, maximum out-of-pocket, or other specifications that could financially cripple entire families.

Research studies have found that more than 66% of bankruptcies were related to medical issues.[3] These bankruptcies may have been caused by the high cost of care or the time the person was simply unable to work. 530,000 families turn to bankruptcy every year and a majority of those are due to medical related challenges.

The greater the financial burden, the greater the risk of bankruptcy, further increasing stress. And even though people may go through bankruptcy, if they don't learn from their mistakes, they're bound to repeat them again, slipping them right back into the cycle.

---

3   https://www.cnbc.com/2019/02/11/this-is-the-real-reason-most-americans-file-for-bankruptcy.html

All this financial pressure, stress, and anxiety will increase mortality rates. As financial issues are the number-one cause of stress, stress is linked to six of the deadliest diseases: heart disease, cancer, lung disease, accidents, cirrhosis of the liver, and suicide.

Money-related issues are literally killing millions of Americans every year.

When you boil it down, this financial crisis that's affecting millions of people every single day isn't *just* about money, it's a deadly health crisis. And it affects more people than all other diseases *combined*.

DAMAGED RELATIONSHIPS

Financial issues are the number one reason long-term relationships and marriages fail. In my experience, in every situation I've witnessed, these problems led to dishonesty, deception, and outright lies. A person who's feeling the direct pressure of financial stress may worry what his or her partner, husband or wife, or family is going to think of them and their failures, so they start hiding the truth.

How many times have you seen movies or TV shows depicting an individual who has been out of work for months and their spouse has no idea? Those situations are believable because they happen – and they happen every single day.

People wake up in the morning, act like everything's alright, and meanwhile the late notices from their mortgage lender, the shutoff notices from the electrical company, cable bills, credit cards, and so on are either tossed in the garbage or stuffed deep into a drawer in their home office. They go about putting every purchase on whatever credit card they can get their hands on now and, in time, there won't be any more available credit upon which to live.

This play-acting causes distrust, frustration, and fights. Those fights become personal. I've seen this in my office too many times – those personal fights begin to wound, and with enough time, the damage becomes too much and the relationship fractures beyond repair.

WHY DO WE HAVE SO MUCH TROUBLE UNDERSTANDING MONEY?

Much of the problem that establishes a poor belief set about money and finances is a *lack of proper education.*

According to Forbes, two-thirds of Americans couldn't pass a basic financial literacy test. If you feel you're in that group, it's not your fault.

What did you learn in school about money?

Do you remember any class in high school that was specifically devoted to financial literacy?

Can you recall any type of actual educational effort made on the part of your school that focused on your financial life?

The only thing I remember from my Home Economics class I took in the 8th grade was how to make chili and sew a pillow. I can still remember our teacher refused to try our chili because she thought we may have poisoned it. I will admit, knowing how to make chili came in handy in college, but it didn't do anything to help me survive in real life.

Most of us can't recall these financial literacy classes because they didn't exist. Even today, even after so many financial disasters have struck this country, we don't have a public education system that establishes financial literacy early in life. I have my theories, too; I strongly feel this is done on purpose and it's criminal in my opinion.

Think about this: If you wanted to create a population that didn't think outside the box, that did what the government told them to do, a lot like robots (go.to.school, get.a.job, pay.your.taxes), and after 40 years retire on the *hope* that they'll actually have the pension they were promised (which is becoming less and less likely in numerous states), Social Security (they paid into but which has been raided again and again to pay for other pet projects the political elite force on us), and maybe some money in a 401(k), the school system would probably look a lot like the one we have today.

It would be a population where most of the citizens go through life financially illiterate, who predominantly live paycheck to paycheck, regardless of their actual income, and live in a constant state of financial stress, anxiety, and fear.

In order to create that kind of population, you'd start early in life … with the exact same educational system we have today.

> **65% of people are considered financially illiterate**

It's been my opinion for a long time that the education system is designed to keep the population financially ILLITERATE. It's no mistake, when you consider 65% of people are considered financially illiterate. Why else would this vitally important subject, the subject of money, be completely ignored in our schools? As I said earlier, it's criminal. So, if you feel you're one of those 65% who has little to no financial knowledge, it's not your fault.

How else can one explain the most important subject in life being completely ignored?

Most of us are living paycheck to paycheck and are so rooted in our belief systems because we didn't have the right educational system to guide us and we never realize it's a problem …

… until it's too late.

We also are bombarded by external influences. Social media, Google, YouTube, television, newspapers, magazines, radio, podcasts, etc., are all specifically designed to capture your attention, make you feel inadequate, and make you feel as though someone else has the answers.

The answers always cost money.

So, we dump mountains of money chasing after hope, solutions, more "stuff" or business ideas we *think* will fulfill us, make us happy, or make us rich. We watch the rich and famous and do our best to emulate their lifestyle. We rack up more and more credit card debt in order to be someone we're not. In the end, we end up using money to dull our pain not fulfill our purpose.

I would also say, as a society, it appears we are spiritually lost. The term I use here, "*spiritually*," refers not to a religious belief system but rather to the spirit or being of an individual. Most of us wander around looking to external sources to fill some kind of void in our lives, something that isn't quite right, a reason why we aren't happy.

When we're spiritually lost – when we feel as though something is lacking in our lives, in our marriages, in our jobs – we often look to something material to fill it. I see this often with my clients.

Finally, when we do turn to "experts" for answers, such as the financial industry, we think we're on the right track, but far too often they're more focused on selling products or services, which only perpetuates the cycle. Given what's happening in today's society, a mutual fund or an annuity is not the answer to people's problems. The issue is rooted much deeper than what people think and therefore needs an entirely different approach.

We are, in a real sense, caught in a trap.

But please do not despair. I want you to have hope. There is a solution, and it may not be as far off as you think. No matter your financial situation, your job, your income, or anything else, you can get out of this vicious, dangerous cycle.

The more we understand about how people process information, how our beliefs are formed, and how those beliefs trickle down into excuses, and then into actions, and ultimately into results – the B.E.A.R. Trap – the more we're in a position to make meaningful, lasting changes.

My company investigates these things and with cooperation, support from other experts, and amazing discoveries about the brain – how people process information and how a lack of valuable information and education can and often does affect many aspects of our lives – we are positioned to provide the best support and resources to help you overcome the challenges and struggles you face. Our mission is to help people transform their beliefs, their relationship with money, in a nonjudgmental and meaningful way.

Remember, information does not lead to transformation. You can go through any point-by-point system that teaches you *how* to pay down your debt, invest your income, etc.… but if you don't address your fundamental belief system, you'll constantly be falling back into the B.E.A.R. Trap.

DON'T DESPAIR

I've seen just about every kind of situation a financial advisor could imagine. I've seen couples with everything going for them crash and burn. I've seen seniors reach retirement, having taken all the right basic steps, only to discover they'll be scraping by for the rest of their lives.

Powerful men and women chase the wrong things, buy the wrong properties and cars and furniture and toys and get so deep into debt that bankruptcy is the only way out.

I've studied the patterns and behaviors, listened to the same advice you've heard for years, and even provided the same surface-level step-by-step guides intended to get you out of debt or moving toward a solid retirement portfolio. But everywhere you look, we're getting deeper and deeper into debt, mired in a financial mess.

It's not getting better.

So many things go wrong. So many mistakes are made at almost every level so that when a man, woman, or couple finds financial success and finally shifts from the "poor" or "struggling middle class" label to "rich," they often don't have the right tools to manage their finances properly and maintain their newfound wealth. Unfortunately, many will end up right back where they started: financially drowning, struggling, and stressed.

They stumble along, buying a new house to impress friends and family, a new car to look the part of the successful businessperson or real estate agent or fill-in-the-blank, they splurge on extravagant luxury vacations. They can never have enough designer bags or jewelry or high-end clothing and they must have the newest smartphone or tablet and the latest and greatest flat screen television. They'll attend the "free chicken dinner" hosted by a local financial advisor and within a few minutes of the presentation decide this is the person they'll turn all their hard-earned money over to.

They'll pay this newfound financial advisor good money to set up a plan, tell them where to invest, what to save, and how to do it, and then quickly say to their new advisor, "Just take care of this for me" without a second thought.

Somewhere along the way, they'll drift off the path. They'll take a shift left when they should have gone straight. They'll misread the stars or the trees or they'll ignore the guide altogether. They should have stayed on the path, but their temptations get the best of them and they end up making bad decision after bad decision until it's too late.

Walking along, paying more attention to the wrong temptations, these "rich" aren't focused on *the steps* around them. Their focus is on *the view*: the nice car, the gorgeous house, the massive flat screen, the backyard toys and the here-and-now things they thought mattered. One bad step, one mistake – one simple change in tax policy or the stock market or the real estate market or interest rates or out of control government debt or the pending pension crisis, a foreign war in a country they've never heard of, or a medical bombshell they never anticipated – and *snap!* They're caught.

A bear trap is a brutal device that ensnares anyone who wanders into its grip. The first thing you feel is pressure. Sudden, fierce, definitive pressure. Somewhere north of the ankle, depending on the size of the trap, a jagged metal bar bites into the meaty muscle of the leg. Within a moment, you feel a sting shoot up through your entire body.

Then, in a panic, you wake up to realize the agonizing truth: you're caught.

Where did it all go wrong?

Where *does* it all go wrong?

You're about to discover 10 reasons everything can go wrong. 10 reasons the *rich go broke. 10 reasons why everyone goes broke and stays broke.*

PART TWO
THE TOP 10 REASONS

THE

RICH
GO BROKE

CHAPTER 6

Reason One:
Empty Rooms, Packed Garage

From age 10 on, I mowed lawns, raked leaves, weeded, and trimmed hedges. During college I upgraded my job title and took a job as a "landscaper" which is a glorified term describing everything I had been doing prior, which is mowing lawns, raking leaves, weeding, and trimming hedges. At first it was simply a job, a way to make extra money. Never in my wildest dreams did I think it would have such a lasting impression on me.

How wrong I was.

One day my boss and I were headed to my favorite house. This was different. It was this one house that changed everything about me – my life, my thinking, and my future.

It wasn't the entire house, mind you. It was one room.

One empty room.

Oh, and one stuffed garage … these were the things that struck me and stuck with me through the years.

The sun slammed the top of my head. I'd forgotten my hat, and to my regret I never used sunscreen. The temperature was flirting with 90, and it was still early in the season. The Ford van rumbled down the main thoroughfare, the radio fixed on a talk show as it always was. At 21 or 22, I tolerated it. My boss loved it.

The van was loaded with equipment ranging from walk-behind

mowers to backpack blowers to weed trimmers to an assortment of gardening tools, all clattering and clanging with each hump and bump and snag in the asphalt. We slowed and turned off the main street, climbed a hill, and made another turn, the groaning wheels protesting my boss's sharp angles.

We entered a relatively new community. New lawns struggled to take root in hard, rock-strewn soil amid the intense heat. A few already had extravagant sprinkler systems in place, two spraying precious water everywhere – on the grass, mud, sidewalks, driveway, and road. One stream struck us as we drove past, and I relished the ever-so-brief cooling.

The van sidled up to a curb and a familiar house whose lawn I took great pride working on. We'd been cutting the grass there every other week since the beginning of the year. My boss knew the owners, but I had yet to see anyone here.

The house was impressive. In fact, this wasn't any ordinary house – this was an *estate.* With a stunning view of the ocean, this three-story home was something straight out of a magazine. Gorgeous floor to ceiling wrap-around windows, a three-car garage, an oversized children's playset in the back, and a couple of solar panels on the roof. I rolled the first mower off the ramp and set to trim out the lawn before heading to the backyard. During one of my passes around the house I spotted a late model BMW, perhaps a 7 Series, pulling out of the driveway as the garage bay shut.

Gorgeous, I thought as I squeezed the handle to turn the mower in the opposite direction. *How do people do it? What do all these people do for a living?*

I couldn't figure it out. It seemed these "McMansions," as they were called in the early 1990s, were popping up everywhere. Communities of houses "starting in the $750Ks" seemed to be the norm.

I envied those people. I never used to growing up, but when you're in college and struggling to make something of yourself and being bombarded by ads for the best of the best of everything, you start to feel dejected about where you are and what you (don't) have.

Vaulted ceilings. Four or five bedrooms. Pools, Jacuzzi tubs, waterfalls. Three-and-a-half baths. Large decks for entertaining guests. A big yard. In Hawaii! These things were the latest in an endless parade of must-haves for those with the means.

Or the "means" to get a loan.

What wasn't there to love and envy? This was *the* American Dream, wasn't it? Living like a king was what most of my friends dreamt about while slogging through a chemistry or biology or calculus class. Some figured they'd get there as entrepreneurs, surgeons, lawyers, or actors. Others just assumed wealth was a gift meant for the ones who worked the hardest and were the smartest.

If that were the case, shouldn't I have been on that road? Instead, I was just scraping by each week.

Frankly, at my age I didn't have much to worry about. Living in Hawaii, playing rugby on the weekends, going to school for that business degree, spending time at the beach with no serious responsibilities to think about – what wasn't to enjoy? Then again, I was intent on enjoying my 20s, not thinking about where my life would be in 10, 20, and certainly not in 40 years.

But here – running behind a machine, cutting someone else's lawn with nice, straight lines – I wanted to know the secret. I would soon be grabbing the backpack blower from the van and clearing any evidence of grass clippings from the driveway.

I decided to ask my boss, "Hey, Larry, what do these people do for a living?"

His expression told me something important was about to be said. He stopped and shut down his gas-powered string trimmer, which we had nicknamed *The Beast.* He glanced toward the house and then back at me.

"You want what they've got?" he said.

I nodded absently. Sure. Who wouldn't?

"I want to know how all these people do it," I said.

"Go up on the deck. Look in the windows. Tell me what you see."

I thought he was joking.

"I'm serious. Go. Look."

"That's … weird. What if they – "

"I know the owners well. I can assure you no one's home. Go. Look."

Reluctantly, I did as ordered. I walked across the front lawn, onto the overheating driveway, into the sliver of shade provided by the garage, and along the back. I climbed the 15 steps up onto the deck. It was almost bare. The first thing I saw was two white plastic outdoor chairs and a cheaper end table that sat in the center looking more like a cardboard box standing on its side.

There was no grill. No high-end patio furniture. No evidence of life aside from that cheap outdoor furniture that resembled my own apartment furnishings.

I approached the tinted glass windows, expecting a shout from inside followed by a scream, as though I were some kind of peeping Tom.

My nose inched closer to the glass as my hands cupped around my eyes. Inside I could make out a large kitchen, barren of any appliances aside from a roll of paper towels and a coffee pot. The dining room right in front of me held two more plastic chairs.

Across the dining room was what I presumed to be the living room, but its only fixtures was a giant television and a futon mattress with a crumpled up blanket pressed against the far wall. That was it. It appeared as if they were just moving in.

When I returned, Larry was already in the truck and ready to move on to the next house. I asked him how long they'd been living there. *Had to be only a matter of weeks,* I thought.

"Over a year," he said.

I didn't have a response. It didn't make sense.

As Larry fired up the engine to head to the next job, he explained. "Robert's a political consultant. Sheila's a Realtor®. They seem to do well enough, but he was out of work for two years before finally landing a new job last year. The high powered politician he supported got into some legal trouble and lost the election. Suddenly he was scrambling to find something else. They had the credit, so they bought their dream home and all the toys to go along with it, then Sheila got cancer. The problem is they took a huge mortgage on their home, exhausted their credit cards and spent every dime they had on material items. When Sheila got sick they had no choice but to start selling stuff."

"Do they still live here?" I said.

"They're in hiding. Hiding from collectors. They're living in the basement of Sheila's sisters house. They're unemployed and now in the process of filing for bankruptcy. And now with Sheila's medical bills piling up they're in a dire situation. In fact, because Robert and Sheila have been long time friends of mine and I feel horrible for Sheila I'm doing their landscaping as a favor."

Larry then leaned in and said, "John, you have a bigger net worth than they do."

I thought to myself, Wow, that's really pathetic!

"But they drive a high-end Beemer," I said.

"So?" My boss looked at me at a red light. "Do you think what a person drives or how big their house is tells you anything about their finances?"

I reluctantly admitted that yes, I did.

"Then you'd be surprised. Most of the people in those big houses driving fancy cars can barely afford them. They're one week from defaulting on their loans, and if someone loses their job, they lose the house and the cars and everything else."

I didn't believe him. Not completely. Were people that concerned about outward appearances they would jeopardize their homes, their marriages, their families, their livelihood just to impress a few friends, neighbors, or family?

Would I?

It was that last question that lingered.

My boss went on to say, "John, most of the houses we work on, those people are in a similar situation. You just wouldn't know it looking from the outside.

"Most people I know put up a façade, they're living a false life, not who they really are – they're pretending to be something they're not."

What he said next I'll never forget, it was an old saying, but until that time I never heard it. "Everyone's just trying to keep up with the Joneses – but the Joneses are broke as well!"

A few weeks later, I was taking care of that lawn by myself. As I came around the corner of the house with my mower, I saw a big, burly man at the front door, smacking it, ringing the bell, and peering in through the side panel windows. After a few minutes, he approached me with a swagger of arrogance and, more disconcerting, anger. I stopped the mower.

"You live here?" he shouted at me.

"Uh, no," I said, glancing at the van and all the equipment on the sidewalk.

"You know these people?" He jabbed a finger at the house.

"Nope. Only seen them once. My boss takes care of that stuff."

His demeanor changed. He relaxed. He shook his head. "I own the construction company that built their rock wall. They owe me a lot of money. You see 'em, let 'em know I was here, will you?"

I nodded and told him, "Sure."

Suddenly what my boss had confided started adding up, though I still struggled to believe it.

As if to hammer the point home shortly after the "gentleman" left, surprisingly Robert pulled in as I was blowing off the driveway. Perhaps it was an accident or he just didn't care, but he opened the third bay to his garage, and what I saw has stayed with me to this day.

Bags and bags and bags of trash, from floor to ceiling. They completely filled the garage bay and spilled halfway into the middle one.

The door closed shortly afterward as he probably realized he'd pressed the wrong button. As I shut down the blower, he walked over to me.

"Hey, is Larry here?"

I told him I was alone today. He said okay, he'd call him later.

Larry told me later that the reason the garage bay was full of trash was because they couldn't even afford the garbage collection fees.

Looking back, I could not have been more grateful for this experience.

People are chasing an image rather than substance

Makes me think about how many golden lessons lurk in every situation and encounter we experience. It was here that I realized that many people are chasing an image rather than substance. They're living paycheck to paycheck while the exterior of their house and possessions boast of wealth. They spend a fortune to look a certain way, but at the end of the day, it's a house of cards, ready to collapse with the slightest breeze.

What I saw at that house hit home and lead me to a revelation to change not only my life, but an entire industry in the process. This experience was a transformational moment that gave me a completely different perspective that thankfully changed my life forever. It made me realize never be fooled by what you see on the outside because on the inside it's often a different story.

Beautiful exteriors and phony realities. So many of us are living that way ... and refuse to see it. We often don't see problems until they run us over; then all we have to look at is the fading bumper and tires that just ran us over!

Trap One:
Stuck on the Outside

 BELIEFS: I need an image in order to impress others no matter the cost or the consequences.

 EXCUSES: "I can't let people know what's really happening." "I need to spend more to be more."

 ACTIONS: Digging in, even when the pressure builds.

 RESULTS: Finding yourself in too deep of a hole to get out. You're Bankrupt.

Have you ever felt like you were on the outside looking in and more than anything you simply wanted to be involved in the group, the club, the experience, the celebration, the laughter, or whatever was taking place behind closed doors? Most of us, at one time or another, have felt as though we were missing out on something.

When you feel stuck on the outside, when you feel as though you're not invited, not welcomed, or there was something wrong with you and you so desperately wanted to be included with the "in" group, was there any thought crossing your mind wondering, "What could I do to make myself welcome to these people?"

What can I do to impress them?

It's easy to get caught up in this idea that the way we look, the car we drive, or even the house we own impresses people. That's because they do.

Sometimes.

But even though these things might impress some family or friends, perhaps even neighbors, it's difficult to keep that façade up for long, especially if your income is limited.

This ***Belief*** is rooted in the ***need to impress others***. What other people think about you can overwhelm your common sense and your ability to think and act rationally.

We often place higher value on outside perceptions than the integrity of our family or finances. It's an easy trap to slip into and can be rooted deep in our past, when we were seeking attention from our parents and were rewarded based on what they saw rather than what was real.

> **We often place higher value on outside perceptions than the integrity of our family or finances.**

The family who had bought this McMansion may have done so for a number of reasons. They had grown children, so perhaps their initial motivation was to purchase a home big enough for their grandkids to visit and play. That's not unreasonable.

However, you don't need a lot of space to raise a family. You need love, support, and encouragement – and certainly food and clothing – but you don't need five or six bedrooms, a game room, a backyard that resembles a waterpark and a massive open floor space where the living, dining, family rooms, and kitchen all join together.

Looking at the outside certainly makes it ***appear*** as though people have everything working for them. You see the pristine lawns, the exotic plants and shrubbery, the oversized deck or properly landscaped patio with gorgeous tables and chairs, the cushions that could hold you comfortably for hours basking outside, the $5,000 playset for the kids, the oversized shed to store all the pool supplies, the fancy cars in the driveway and so forth.

But inside sits an old sofa in the living room. A futon, perhaps. The dining table is draped with a cloth, and underneath is well-worn wood, a scratched surface, and beaten down wicker chairs – products of a desperate tag sale purchase. The kitchen is oversized with a stainless-steel refrigerator, but the utensils are secondhand. The dishes are hand-me-downs, cracked and chipped. The cupboards are stuffed with mac & cheese, ramen noodles, and an assortment of quick canned meals.

There's nothing wrong with those things, mind you, but the more you look around and pay attention to the externals, the more you see the internal issues just beneath the surface.

Quickly thereafter, the recurring *Excuses* kick in and build over time.
"We have to make sure this looks good for our guests."
"We have to get that new dining room set by Christmas."
"They're having a sale and offering 0% financing."
"We've gone this far and can't stop now."
"My next commission at work is going to change everything."
We spend so much time and energy focused on the wrong things, the approval of strangers, neighbors, friends, co-workers, and even family, that we lose sight of what's most important: family and our future.

GETTING CAUGHT

 Beliefs: I need an image to impress others no matter the cost or the consequences. Some may attribute this belief system to insecurity, stretching all the way back to a person's childhood. Others may ascribe it to a sense of bravado or accomplishment that is necessary to succeed in corporate America (look and act like you've made it, and you will). This overwhelming desire to impress outsiders puts us on a hamster wheel of spending that often leads to a complete wipeout economically.

Excuses: "I can't let people know what's really happening."
"I need to spend more to be more." Will you get banned from
the next social gathering? Would your country club pass be
revoked? Might friends and neighbors suddenly start gossiping
about you? All are possible, but the excuses generally involve
what others think of us, and that becomes more important than
what's truly happening in our lives and family.

Actions: Digging in, even when the pressure builds. In order
to maintain a specific external image, people will dig in harder
the tougher financial times become. They do this for one of two
reasons:

1. Because they fear the perception of friends, family,
   neighbors, or colleagues
2. Because they honestly believe the issues are only
   temporary.

Results: Finding yourself in too deep of a hole to get out of.
You're Bankrupt. You can't effectively dig your way out of
a hole by digging deeper. However, that's what we often try
to do when our desire to impress overwhelms reason and we
keep spending, even when we can't afford it, just to keep up
appearances.

INTO THE MIRE

When you look at the stats I mentioned previously regarding how
many people in this country are living paycheck to paycheck, you realize
many of them are just one job loss, medical issue, car breakdown, or home
repair away from a couple months' missed mortgage payments and losing
everything.

The people who owned this house were struggling, and they had been
for quite some time. Life became an intense struggle and soon they were
hiding from bill collectors, even belligerent collection agents. It got to
the point that they had to begin tossing their garbage in the garage. At

first, it was just temporary, just for "a few weeks, until we can get things back on track." But those few weeks passed, and before they realized it, months had transpired and their garage turned into a trash dump. And soon thereafter, Robert and Sheila were hiding out in a basement.

The *Actions* this family took simply forced them to focus on their image rather than the internals: the family, their marriage, the job and their health. They continued to press forth with this desire to have the oversized house they honestly didn't need, even to the point where losing it (along with everything else) was a real possibility.

During the heat of summer, they couldn't afford to run the air conditioner, so they had to grin and bear the stench of all that garbage piling up in the garage, floor to ceiling; they got used to it and didn't even realize how much it smelled throughout the rest of the house, and since no one was allowed to visit – no one could tell them how bad it'd become.

As far as the lawn care, they didn't have the equipment to do it themselves; that's why they continued to ask my boss to do it for them. Unfortunately for my boss, he wasn't getting paid, either. He still had to pay me and the other person working with us. He had been friends with this person growing up, so he wanted to do whatever he could to help.

By the end of the summer, the bill for the landscaping and lawn services was well over $3,000. It was a write-off as it would never be paid. It didn't bother Larry because he wanted to help his friends. This turned out to be another great lesson I learned as well.

The *Results* were financial devastation. Plain and simple. So much could have been salvaged, including their reputation, but they couldn't get unstuck, and once they began down that road, they kept digging in and holding out hope.

They could've given up on that six-bedroom, 3,500-square-foot home, but *they didn't want to*. They didn't want their friends, their neighbors, their family, their coworkers, or whoever to view them as failures.

The only failure was failing to admit what was so clear to those on the outside: that they were in over their heads. As Ryan Holiday and Stephen Hanselman point out in *The Daily Stoic Journal,* simply owning things is expensive: "The cost of an item isn't simply what it's sold for, but what it costs the owner to own. So much of our desire for material goods comes at the great price of both anxiety and the loss of our serenity – and even when gained, these things often leave us more anxious and less serene."

> **"The cost of an item isn't simply what it's sold for, but what it costs the owner to own. So much of our desire for material goods comes at the great price of both anxiety and the loss of our serenity – and even when gained, these things often leave us more anxious and less serene."**

In this situation, it would've been better to immediately recognize the problem and not assume he was going to find a job within a few months. Maybe he could have. Maybe everything would have been fine, but they got in deeper and deeper. As a result the interest and late fees compounded. Even though he ultimately found a job with another politician, it was in another city and state. They had to sell the house, anyway, and move.

By that time, though, they were so deep in debt that the sale basically went to pay off what they owed. According to my boss, they couldn't buy a new house because their credit had bottomed out and they had no savings to speak of. They struggled to find a quality rental and basically started over with nothing, not even decent furniture, all at the age of 55.

Sometimes old furniture is comfortable. Sometimes that ratty, well-worn leather couch you picked up for $50 at a local tag sale or thrift store is just perfect. What's more important? What other people think of you? Or having a future where you don't have to stress every single day about who's calling, pounding on your door, or whether this is the week your bank decides to foreclose?

Being smart with money isn't about giving up your plasma TV or your daily latte. It's about setting priorities, managing expectations and always focusing on the long term consequences of your decisions. If you're constantly focusing on things you *think* will impress others, you will be setting yourself for some hard times in the future because there will *always* be something bigger, better, and more expensive to buy.

I heard a quote some time ago and it ties in perfectly with the message here:

Rich people stay rich by living like they're broke. Broke people stay broke by living like they're rich.

In my many years of counseling, one of the reoccurring and consistent reasons people suffer financially is this desperate need to use money they don't have, to buy things they don't need, in order to impress people who really don't care about them in the first place. People have convinced themselves that their outward appearance to the world is what they need to do in order to succeed. It's this Belief that's killing people. Once you can eliminate this Belief in your own mind, you'll be setting yourself up for a successful future.

> **Rich people stay rich by living like they're broke. Broke people stay broke by living like they're rich.**

YOUR TURN

Now it's time to look inward. Be introspective. Pull out your guidebook and complete Activity #4. Be introspective. Be honest.

Take your time. You'll discover as you work through the guidebook activities that your answers may change. That's not a problem.

Just continue to be honest as you work.

CHAPTER 7

Reason Two:
I Trust My Advisor

Afternoon had rolled in, along with a decent drenching from a passing storm. I was taking a moment to glance out of my home office window, spotting the dark gray clouds fleeing into the distance. It was Friday and I was working from home. At the time I was living in California, and these storms would normally bring some relief from the humidity, but not this one. It wasn't so hot that I needed to keep the AC pumping, but that might soon change, I thought. Steam rolled up from the driveway and formed a thin cloud that hovered. I knew the time to close up the windows had come.

As I stood, my phone chirped. That wasn't unusual. I was a financial advisor – clients and prospects called all the time. But instead of closing up the windows first, my hand snatched at the handset.

"Good afternoon," I said.

At first all I heard was raspy breathing.

"Hello?"

"John." An old voice with barely any strength stretched through the line. I strained to match that voice with a face. "Bill?"

Bill was an old friend of mine, a man who was quick with a good, clean joke or a humorous comment. He was jovial and generous, sometimes to a fault. Bill was sharp, even into his late 70s. He had worked hard, saved, invested well, and had a rock solid retirement fund. He was a member at a local athletic club, and if someone thought they could take him down on the tennis court, they'd be in for quite a surprise.

I always considered Bill to be this strong, indomitable man far younger than his actual years on this earth, but that day his voice conveyed something I never would have associated with him: fear.

He was terrified, and my first thought was that he'd suffered some medical emergency. But why call me? He had a lot of friends throughout the community. I loved the guy and would certainly do whatever I could to help, but I wasn't the best option if he were suffering a heart attack.

"Yeah, John, listen," he said. "I got a serious problem."

My legs eased me down into my chair, the rising humidity no longer on my mind. "What is it?"

He paused. Hesitation, perhaps? Not sure how to form the right words? When he finally spoke, he uttered words I would never forget.

"My advisor won't give me my money."

My first instinct was that Bill had gotten confused or perhaps misunderstood his advisor. This didn't make sense at all. Financial advisors get to know one another in time and build a sort of community. Sure, as a professional, you're in competition, but there's generally enough work for everyone. So long as you're honest and have integrity, you'll build good relationships and even friendships with your colleagues.

> **"My advisor won't give me my money."**

So when someone in my profession hears those words from anybody – longtime friend or not – it stings, and you get this building pressure in your gut.

"What do you mean? Who?"

"I'm supposed to meet him in an hour," Bill said. His voice – weak, distant, and carrying every bit his age when I had first answered the phone – now sounded even frailer, shell-shocked, even. "Can you get here?"

As my eyes scanned the calendar on my desk, I scrolled through the one in my mind. I didn't have anything pressing. "Sure," I said, "I'll be there."

"There" was the health club. Bill spent much of his days down at the club. If he wasn't smashing a tennis ball into oblivion, he was sharing drinks, memories, or advice with any number of other members. Bill was the kind of guy who could easily adopt the title "Mayor" and no one would question it.

My drive to the club was about 30 minutes with traffic. The town where I lived and worked was a close-knit community, but the athletic club was closer to a major business hub, so it was a bit of a drive. I kept the windows up while thoughts swirled in my head.

I got to the club about 15 minutes before Bill said this advisor would meet him. I was let in and spotted Bill at a table in the restaurant area. What looked like a small glass of scotch on the rocks sat sweating next to his shaking hand. It looked as though it hadn't been touched. In Bill's hands were a couple sheets of paper rattling in his grip.

"Bill," I said softly, not wanting to startle him.

He saw me but didn't *see* me for a few moments. I stood, awkward, feeling the heaviness of the moment press on me. Finally, he snapped out of whatever journey his mind had dragged him on and offered me a seat.

"Thanks for coming, John."

"No problem. Now, tell me, what's going on?"

I eased into the seat and scanned the table. A stack of loose papers spread across it like a cover, a tablecloth – this type of scene was far too familiar to me. When you're a financial advisor long enough, you get used to scattered pages of documents in no discernible order, some handwritten notes, printouts, and statements. Too often this is all one big mess, but Bill was a bit more organized than that.

"John," Bill said, setting down the page he had been holding, "I can't figure it out. This guy's been helping me for several years and I thought everything was going well. But I asked for my RMD and he balked."

The RMD is the required minimum distribution from an Individual Retirement Account (IRA). Anyone over 70 ½ years of age is required to withdraw a predetermined amount out of their IRA every year.

"I asked again and he said he'd get it to me tomorrow," he said. "That was two weeks ago, John. That was the last time I spoke with him as he refuses to answer and return my calls. I hadn't seen him down here either at the club for two weeks, so I finally confronted him at his home."

Bill struggled for the next words. I prodded him, gently.

"He said he'd meet me here." Bill checked for the watch that wasn't wrapped around his wrist. "At three." He shrugged. "I have no idea what time it is."

"Just about three," I said.

He turned and scanned the dining facility. Men and women occasionally strolled through, on their way to the gym or tennis courts or to play racquetball or to the lockers or to some other destination. It was relatively quiet. Typical for this time of day in the middle of the week.

A couple things stuck out from his statement. First, Bill was 78, and if he'd been using this advisor for several years, that means he should have been getting this RMD each year previous. If he wasn't, that led to my second concern: Why would he have waited this long to press the advisor for more detailed information?

Neither question was all that pressing in light of Bill's distress.

"Who is it?" I asked.

"Huh?" Bill appeared surprised. He seemed to have forgotten I was there for a moment. He might have been replaying the past four or some-odd years since he'd handed over the majority of his retirement fund to this advisor, wondering if there were signs he had missed, if he'd forgotten a stipulation or an agreement he'd made. When times get tough, one of the first things people do is try to figure out what went wrong.

Sometimes *what went wrong* has a simple answer. Sometimes it's intensely complicated. In truth, it doesn't really matter, because none of us get to go back and undo the mistakes we made. The only thing we can do is move forward, learn from them, and begin to change our processes (or *beliefs*) to avoid a repeat.

When I held Bill's attention, I asked again, "Who is it?"

"Who's who?"

The poor man was simply lost. I felt terrible. I loved this guy. He was a wonderful friend, great all-around guy, and kind soul. Seeing him like this was so out of character it was hard to witness. I supposed it would be like visiting your father after a few years and seeing a broken, frail, weak man struggling to simply lift his aging frame up from a chair or walk down the hall when on your last visit he was zipping up and down a ladder, running errands like a linebacker, and showing no signs of doubt for his physical capabilities.

"The advisor," I said gently.

"Oh. Stephen. Nichols. Stephen Nichols."

My face had to convey the shock I felt. Steve Nichols? I knew the man. I'd known him for much of my life. I ran high school track with his brother. The guy practically lived at this health club, but he was a highly respected member of the community, a youth coach, and an awesome person. People loved Steve Nichols. Steve's infectious smile is the one thing I always remembered about him.

But an advisor?

As I said, financial professionals tend to know one another, especially in smaller communities, if not personally then at least by name. *Stephen Nichols* was never a name that I'd crossed paths within this industry.

"Coach Steve?" I asked.

Bill nodded.

Steve had been inducted into the athletic hall of fame for basketball at my high school. He was a legend. And a pretty good tennis player. I suppose that might have been how Bill and Steve had gotten to talking about investments and financial advice: during a game. The seeds of so many business decisions and partnerships are planted during competitive endeavors.

For everything I knew about Steve, never in a million years would I have imagined him as a financial advisor.

"Can I see the statements?" I asked.

Bill scanned the room once more as he handed me a typed sheet of paper. There were four years' worth of papers he had here, actually. 16 statements. Four years' worth of quarterly statements. The typeface was odd. There was no official letterhead. No logo. Just paper that had been run through a traditional typewriter. These sheets contained Bill's name, address, and other contact information. No account number and no other identifying information.

Below the personal information was a starting and ending balance. I'm good with numbers and as I flipped through these pages I began to suspect something – something that shouldn't be.

I whipped out a calculator from my pocket and started punching numbers. I felt that familiar sinking feeling creep in. I knew what had happened. I didn't need to be a forensic investigator. I didn't need to know more about what was talked about, what was promised, or anything between Bill and Steve. The numbers told the truth.

"4%," I said.

Bill's jaw set as he studied me.

"Right. A good return."

I set the pages down to study my friend.

"No, Bill. Four *percent*."

He wasn't following. He was focused on how much he should be getting back from these investments with Steve.

"Each of these statements shows exactly a 4% return. Every quarter."

"Isn't that a good thing?"

"Listen to me, Bill. Please. No investment account ever returns exactly the same amount every quarter, much less every year. None. They fluctuate."

I couldn't tell if Bill was beginning to understand, but he was likely straining to draw hope out of what I could already tell was nearly hopeless. I needed him to reach the point of truth. I didn't want to be the one to break this news to him, so I asked questions.

"There's no mention of a financial institution. Do you know it?"

A slight shake of his head.

"Do you know the investments?"

"What do you mean?"

"There's no list of investments. No information about where your money was to be gaining these returns."

He could only stare at me, helpless. Bill rifled through the papers and managed to free a small scrap of paper, handwritten, from the pile.

"Here," he said, handing it to me.

"What is it?" I asked as I took it.

"A list. My investments. With … him."

I scanned it. It was a handwritten list of U.S. Treasury bonds. This wasn't a list of investments. Certainly not the kind that would merit 4% returns every quarter! I had no desire to raise the heat in this man's life, but I was feeling every bit as angry as Bill was terrified.

"Bill, you're a smart man. You know investments."

He studied me. No argument.

"How do you return 4% every quarter with U.S. treasuries in this low interest rate environment?"

"I know, I know. I always thought that was strange."

I wanted to say, "You 'thought that was strange,' but you didn't do anything about it?" But Bill didn't need berating. He needed help.

"Did you write a check for your initial investment to the advisor or to a known and reputable financial institution?"

"To the advisor."

"What did he charge you to manage this money?"

Bill's head shook.

"Nothing."

None of this made any sense. Not any sense *in light of legitimate advisors and investments*. I already knew but wanted to be certain that this was fraud. Across the board. From start to finish.

"I was getting my RMD each year," Bill chimed in, a bit of hope still clinging to his shoulders and the weight was tearing him down.

My head bobbed on its own as I began drawing forth more of the paperwork dividing the two of us. Three o'clock had now come and gone. I knew Steve wouldn't show. I knew what had happened.

"But not now," I said.

"I told you, he won't even return my calls. I had to track him down just to get him to meet."

Looking around, I said, perhaps a bit too firmly, "And where is he? What credentials does he have? What firm does he work for? Where does he custody the assets?"

Bill held up a quavering hand. "Stop," he begged. "Please stop."

He knew. Whatever had caused him to jump into financial bed with this man, a person who apparently marketed himself as an "advisor" – something I actually *was,* and a profession I and most of the rest of my peers took and take seriously – Bill knew he'd been taken advantage of.

"She doesn't know." His voice had become little more than a whisper.

I leaned a bit closer. "What?"

"My wife. She doesn't know." He was in serious trouble and knew it. What he had invested with Stephen Nichols had been the bulk of his and his wife's retirement savings. He was visibly shaking. I struggled to console him but to no avail. A man of his age … I began counting the medical emergencies that could happen at any moment. I knew a little then about the impact prolonged and intense sudden stress has on the body, the heart, the brain, and how it affected millions of Americans.

I was seeing that stress play out before me in the visage and body language of a dear old friend. I felt terrible, but more than that I felt angry. I wasn't the one betrayed, but I might as well have been for how I hated Steve Nichols in that moment. All I could think about was his big cheesy smile.

We sat in relative silence for a time, the glass of scotch now devoid of its rocks. A waitress meandered close on a couple of occasions, and while Bill couldn't or wouldn't look up at her, I begged her off with a slight wave as politely as I could. She smiled and gave us space.

3:30, and no sign of Steve, but Bill spotted someone else. Thomas. A 60-something gentleman of some business and political stature in the community. Bill waved him over.

"Thomas, this is John," Bill introduced us, and we shook hands. "John, Thomas introduced me to Steve." Turning to Thomas, Bill said in a trembling tone, "Have you seen him lately?"

Thomas put his hands out in surrender. He didn't know, but I could tell he knew something about the situation. Perhaps, I surmised, he'd already been burned by Stephen Nichols. Thomas said, "I know nothing" and quickly walked away. It was clear to me he knew *everything.*

Two hours later and that single scotch finally drained, Bill and I parted ways. I struggled with what had happened. Bill didn't really know Steve well. He'd gotten a referral from Thomas and, after asking around, he had heard good things about the man. The common refrain I would hear in the weeks and months that followed were, "I trusted him."

Neither Bill nor the other dozen or so people who had "invested" with Stephen Nichols had questioned his education, credentials, or integrity.

They'd trusted him.

I called Bill the next day to check in and asked how things were going.

He snapped back.

"How do you think it's going?"

Fair enough.

I managed to squeeze out that Stephen had agreed to meet with his attorney on Friday. That didn't bode well and Bill knew it, but there was hope – hope of recovering at least *some* of what had been lost.

Bill asked if I would accompany him to this meeting. "Of course," I said, and I cleared my schedule.

On Thursday, Stephen Nichols' wife or girlfriend (I'm not sure to this day who she was) found him hanging in their basement. He had been so well-respected throughout the community and a man of influence that the media paid little attention to the people he hurt and the millions he had bilked from unsuspecting "clients." They glossed over the fraud and focused on the "great community-minded leader."

There was no investigation. The news never mentioned suicide. What was lost was lost.

What made matters worse was that the health club had the gall to pay homage to Mr. Nichols. They had several mome nts of silence throughout the day, and they even named a tennis court after him.

Meanwhile, Bill lost everything. He never recovered, financially or emotionally.

And I never forgot it.

"I trust my advisor." Sadly, it's this belief that has caused so many people, so much pain and agony.

Do you trust him with your future? Do you trust him with your life? With your spouse's life?

Such a simple phrase has caused so much harm to thousands of people across the country and throughout time.

"I trust my advisor."

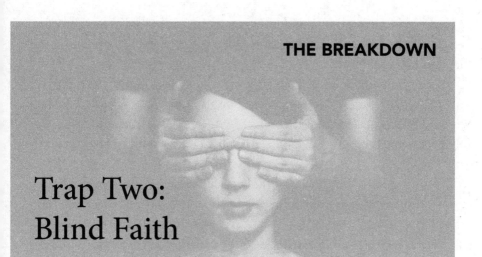

Trap Two: Blind Faith

 BELIEFS: I'm sure that those who call themselves "advisors" are trustworthy.

 EXCUSES: "The referral was all I needed." "I didn't make time to dig deep and I didn't know what to ask."

 ACTIONS: Handing over hard-earned money to a stranger ... and hoping.

 RESULTS: Getting scammed and ripped off and potentially losing everything, including your health and your family.

Blind faith is a dangerous thing. When you have blind faith, you really have no idea what you're getting into.

In this story, my friend Bill had a *Belief* that just because an individual he knew (who was a member at the same health club he attended, was referred by someone else, who *advertised himself as an advisor*) that this was all he needed.

He failed to investigate. He failed to protect his money, to protect his assets from himself, in a sense. Remember, you can go out and hire a financial advisor, but if you don't know anything about them – their education, their experience, their process, their philosophy, their firm, or their trustworthiness – then you're essentially throwing your money at them and hoping for the best. You have no idea of their motivations, their knowledge, or if they can even discern between a sound investment and a risky one.

This is especially important in today's modern environment. The Internet allows anyone to make it *appear* as though they're professional, well-oiled, and experienced. A decent website template can have someone looking legit for a few bucks, but does that mean they are? No, it doesn't. Even if someone says they're an advisor and they have a good-looking website with decent information, it could be copied. The entire thing could be cloned. And you could easily find yourself at the mercy of whoever is taking charge of your finances.

Another thing to consider is that even those who are in fact "licensed" financial advisors may not be "qualified, capable, or effective at managing your financial affairs." It could take someone 6-8 weeks to pass the required exams necessary for someone to call themselves a financial advisor. Compare that to other industry professionals like hairdressers where it could take up to two years to become qualified. Just because someone *says* they're a financial advisor means nothing about their abilities or moralities.

It could take someone 6-8 weeks to pass the required exams necessary for someone to call themselves a financial advisor.

Let me ask you a question. If you have children, would you drop them off at *any* daycare facility, without even learning about its history, experience, safety, security, licenses, etc.? Most parents will at least be diligent enough to find out if it's legitimate or not. No loving parent would simply drop their child off at a person's house who "said" they offered daycare, knowing nothing about them and not having any friends or neighbors who know the person.

It simply doesn't happen.

And I hope it wouldn't.

Yet this is what happens far too often across the country. People like Bill simply take another person's word as a testimony for someone else. "He's a great guy" … "You should see their offices" … "I heard they're a good team" … "She goes to my church" … "He played football at the U of XYZ" … "He played professional football" … "She has a master's degree" …

You might even hear someone say, "My son's friend is an advisor." Then that acquaintance adds, "He's starting his own firm and has a gorgeous office. I'm sure he would give you a great deal."

Sounds decent enough, right? Maybe that son's friend is trustworthy and reliable. Maybe he graduated at the top of his class. Maybe he's been working for a financial firm for two years, gaining tremendous experience. Maybe all of that is true.

Would you still hand over $100,000 to this person without asking questions? Would you hand over $50,000 without an interview? Would you hand over $10,000 to somebody you didn't know, all based on a smooth marketing pitch, a slick website and a comment from someone that he or she is a "great person"?

It's easy to say you wouldn't, but look at the aftermath of Bernie Madoff and so many others who built pyramid schemes, who knew the lingo, who dressed the part, who made the right connections, and who *said the right things*.

Understand this: it's often not really about a person's experience or how many people they work for and how much money they may have made as financial advisors for others that people focus on; *it's about what they say.*

Salespeople, the best of them, can make a great living selling just about anything. Mike Rowe once recounted how he got into the business he became famous for. He was a spokesman for QVC – the television shopping channel. During his initial interview with one of the executives of the company, he presented himself well, answered all the questions the way he should have, and then came to a particular test.

The executive handed him a No. 2 pencil and said, "Sell me this."

Mike studied the pencil for a moment and then went into a long sales pitch about how this really wasn't a pencil but a machine. I'm not going to get into the details of exactly how he sold this person on his ability, but the point is if Mike Rowe could win a coveted job by selling an executive a basic No. 2 pencil, realize there are thousands upon thousands of people out there who have similar talents and have been able to separate people from their money with very little effort.

The men and women who invested with Bernie Madoff were not greedy. Some may argue they were, that they were rich people looking to get richer, but that's really a straw man argument. What's important is that Madoff talked the talk, he looked the part, he walked the walk, and he made the promises they desperately longed to hear.

"I can almost guarantee you over 10% return every single year."

Doesn't that get you excited? Of course it does. If an advisor follows that claim with slick lingo and great references that no one actually checks out – or better yet, references from people you know – why would you even hesitate?

It's still blind faith.

Bill's *Excuses* involved not wanting to be the one person at that health club who questioned the integrity of a man who had an unimpeachable character. Bill went with the flow, so to speak, and that was the problem.

Bill didn't want to look foolish for asking what he thought may be perceived as foolish questions. Bill felt he didn't have the time or the know-how or the questions he *should* be asking. After all, he didn't want to insult Mr. Nichols. And, on top of that, a well-known executive referred him – that's all Bill needed. Besides, he'd see Stephen Nichols all the time at the club, with a smile; why *wouldn't* this be legit?

These excuses led Bill to take destructive *Action* by committing his money to an untested, unproven person who was advertising himself as an advisor.

Bill lost. He was fortunate in that it didn't completely ruin him financially, but it hurt badly. Very badly. In fact it nearly cost him his marriage, his retirement, and his life due to the health issues resulting from the stress it pounded down on him. However, Stephen took a number of people for a lot more. Some people lost everything, simply because they trusted his big smile, his reputation in the community, and the endorsement of other people.

These *Results* can be devastating and they can cause just about anyone to feel violated. Some people never recover.

GETTING CAUGHT

 Beliefs: I'm sure that those who call themselves "advisors" are trustworthy. Between friends and family, we all probably know dozens of so-called experts, but just because your mother or best friend or acquaintance at a fitness club makes a recommendation, don't doubt the obligation that you have to vet their character, *especially* when it comes to your money.

 Excuses: "The referral was all I needed." "I didn't make time to dig deep and I didn't know what to ask." People may expect favors, and if you don't give in right away, they might question your faith in them. One's financial life is their responsibility (no one else's), and when money's on the line, it's best to not be drawn into feeling guilty by asking for references, credentials, and the time to verify everything.

 Actions: Handing over your hard-earned money to a stranger … and hoping. The desire for promised results and rewards can overwhelm reason and temperance. However, without careful consideration, research, and understanding, these actions can and often do lead to unexpected and unintended consequences.

 Results: Getting scammed and ripped off and potentially losing everything, including your health and your family. Some might say, "If you take a gamble with your money and lose, then you deserved to." Stop. No one "deserves" to be ripped off. Con artists and even people with good intentions but no experience are everywhere. When it comes to investing, you run the risk of losing everything when you simply trust your advisor without checking credentials and the merits of their experience. This applies to all areas of your life, not just financial.

If you trust your advisor, that's a wonderful thing. But do you know them? Have they been completely honest and forthright about all their experience, all their education, all their certifications? Have you verified what they told you? Trust without verification is a dangerous path to slip down.

Trust without verification is a dangerous path to slip down.

I don't know how prevalent such deception may be in the financial industry. It certainly exists as we read about it all the time. I've spent a good part of my career training, coaching, and mentoring financial advisors and I will say that 99% of them seemed to be good, well intentioned people who wanted to do the right thing. But without digging into their experience yourself, you will never know. But I do know that among independent contractors, even companies advertising construction services, there are a growing number of people – predominantly men – who use falsified, expired, or stolen license numbers when advertising their services. People hire them to remodel their kitchen, put an addition on their house, or do other major work for their home or business simply because of that license number. They never check their background.

A simple phone call to the state regulatory board could verify whether the person utilizing that license number actually owns it or that it's in good standing. All it would take is a 10-minute phone call, at best, or even an online search.

Some financial advisors can pass just about any background check, can pass the most rigorous interviews, and have all their certifications and licenses in good standing, and they still burn their clients.

So how can you possibly know who to trust?

The same way you would when selecting a daycare provider for your children. This person you're choosing to work with can be the difference between prosperity and poverty, success and failure, peace or pain. You *must* check them out carefully. This person is someone you're entrusting your hard earned money with, your money being a critical and essential tool you've worked your life for – something that you fought every day for through years of hard work to earn and build so that one day you could rely on it to provide the life you always dreamed of. You're not hiring a landscaper or a hairdresser.

> **Remember, the grass and your hair will grow back. That is *not* the case with your money.**

Remember, the grass and your hair will grow back. That is *not* the case with your money.

It's very important that you realize this review is just one small step in your process of identifying the most appropriate and *trusted* advisor for your needs. There are many advisors that show up clean today, but that doesn't mean they'll remain that way in the future.

Call around and see what other people know about that person. Get referrals and call them! Pick up the phone; don't simply rely on email. I realize you'll be getting the names of an advisor's favorite clients, but you'll be surprised what these people admit. Ask them if they know of other clients this advisor has (or had) and call them. Remind yourself of *why* you're doing this. You're trying to identify someone to trust your life savings with and who could be the difference between prosperity or poverty. There should be no excuse when it comes to your financial livelihood, your future, even the future of your family.

It's important for you to understand that selecting the *right* financial advisor is a process. This shouldn't be taken lightly or done overnight. You don't go on one date, propose on the spot, and then get married the next day, do you?

No. You court your potential mate. You learn about her. You get to know him. You want to understand who they *really* are, not just the person they act like on that first or second date. If you invest that kind of time into finding the right life partner, you should certainly check out any prospective advisor, too.

Selecting the person or team doesn't mean your work is done. This is a process that requires ongoing verification. Time passes, things happen, and people change. Remain diligent.

Few things cause me to cringe more than having a client or friend tell me, "John, I'm worried. I trust my advisor, but …"

I've heard it too many times. Protect yourself, your hard-earned money, and your investments by being diligent when you look for a financial advisor.

Because of this story and too many others, I decided to do something about it. I even saw this behavior in my own office when people were willing to hand over their entire life savings to me based on nothing more than a 30-minute meet-and-greet in my office. It always struck me as odd. People didn't know anything, really, about me and they were willing to trust me with everything on the spot based on a simple referral, a newspaper quote, or they saw a clip of me on television.

Not long ago I came across a financial advisor who became quite popular (and famous) for telling people to get out of the stock market just before the collapse in 2008.

His warning in 2007 was spot on. Whether it was based on experience or mere luck, we could debate, but the information and predictions he doles out today tells me it was the latter.

Well, after that incredibly successful call on the market, a lot of people began tuning in to him and his advice. He wrote a book, hosted a podcast, and became a regular on business news channels. Due to his newfound popularity, he set up affiliate advisors across the country and advertised seminars for people to attend.

I went to one to find out what this was all about. I kept hearing about droves of men and women signing up for consultations and opening accounts at an alarming rate. I was in the midst of starting my new business and was curious to know why there was so much appeal.

At the seminar, I mingled with a number of the attendees and discovered they, too, were all but ready and eager to sign up … and that was *before* the presentation started! I was the youngest in that room by at least 20 years. These were all retired seniors who were looking for an advisor to manage their money and protect them from the next market crash. The cost of these services didn't matter.

The gentleman who took the stage was charismatic, commanding, and spoke with a touch of humor. He was good. Impressive. The sales pitch was well formulated; it struck all the right chords and hit all the right notes. The audience was engaged.

Like everyone else, I signed up for the consultation. I was going to see this through. I was very interested in learning about their investment strategy, which, by the way, they would not share at the luncheon until you signed up for a consultation. Fair enough.

When the date arrived, I sat in a waiting room with several of those who were at the seminar. Eager, excited people waiting in anticipation.

Once the meeting started, I quickly found out our local "advisor" had recently gotten her required licenses at another firm but couldn't make it through their training program. She had no real experience.

She practically read from a script.

My first question was, "How's business?"

I have since forgotten the actual numbers, but the amount of money they were bringing in every week was staggering. It was tens of millions of dollars. She confided that it was too much for her to handle and they were expanding their offices to add more advisors.

Given my background, I had a lot of questions– which she didn't much care for. She stumbled through most of the ones I asked, but there were many she couldn't answer at all. None of them were all that complicated; I wasn't trying to trick or trap her. I had serious questions that I wanted answered and she should have been able to answer them quite easily.

"No one's ever asked questions before," she said several times, a bit perplexed. "Are you ready to open an account?" She said that last line with a bubbly enthusiasm.

I asked to see certified and accredited performance statements like any investment firm would provide. Either she couldn't or wouldn't, I'm still not sure. Either way, I was unable to get any verifiable proof of their investment performance.

I asked about the fees and even that was a struggle to get the complete answer. After further probing, I was able to determine their fees were double the industry standard.

I kept thinking to myself, people are turning over all their money to this firm blindly, simply because the founder made one good call on the market eight years ago.

"Are you ready to open an account?" She asked again. This time with an impatient tone in her voice. There were guaranteed customers waiting to write her a check and my allocated time was up and she was done sweating over my questions. Frankly, I could tell she didn't care if I opened an account or not, she wanted me to leave.

Let me be clear: I am not attacking the character, integrity, or intellect of this individual. She was doing what she was trained to do: *follow a script and open an account, rinse and repeat.* And because she was never asked questions before, she was not prepared to answer mine.

Before I gave her my answer, I asked one more thing, "Who was that speaker at the seminar? He was good."

She leaned in close and said in a quiet voice, "Don't tell anyone, but he's not a financial advisor. He's a Hollywood actor."

I said, "Come again. He's a what?" I wasn't expecting that at all. When she restated what she said, I still couldn't believe my ears. I don't know another word to describe my feelings than I was simply stunned.

She continued, "Did you watch the Super Bowl last weekend?"

"Of course, why?"

"He was the lead actor in a commercial for a major pizza chain at halftime," she said with a laugh.

With my jaw dropped and my shoulders sunken, I said goodbye and walked out of there like I had seen a ghost. To this day, I still can't believe this massive investment firm, considered to be one of the best in the country, managing billions of dollars, used or still using Hollywood actors in their seminars. On top of that, not disclosing it to their prospects or clients. It's unconscionable.

An actor. Selling people financial advice. Sending them to a newly certified advisor. It's shocking.

As a result of these observations and the growing realization that so many people simply didn't know **how** to choose the right advisor, I put together a comprehensive process with guidelines and questions to ask with explanations to the questions, that will help guide you as you interview financial advisors.

In it, I lay out a thorough process on how best to interview and identify a financial advisor who's appropriate for your needs. You can access "The Ultimate Guide to Selecting Your Financial Advisor" on my website: johnmacgregor.net. You will also find a direct link in the resource section at the end of this book.

Nothing is foolproof, but the more empowered you are, the more information you have at your disposal, the easier it's going to be to make the **right** decisions when it comes time to hire a financial advisor.

> **Take your time. Ask questions. Dig deep. Your life, your family, your marriage, your health, your happiness, and your wealth may depend on it.**

Whatever you do, be diligent. Do **not** hire someone just because someone recommends them or you saw their website or you saw them quoted in the newspaper or you got a free meal.

Take your time. Ask questions. Dig deep.

Your life, your family, your marriage, your health, your happiness, and your wealth may depend on it.

YOUR TURN

Let's take another look at your life. Keep things in perspective. Pull out your guidebook and complete Activity #5.

This is another opportunity to begin diving deep down to the roots and see how your beliefs are impacting your financial life.

CHAPTER 8

Reason Three:
I Don't Need Advice

Sunlight danced across the rolling waves of the Pacific like diamonds. The temperature hovered somewhere close to perfect. I decided to cruise along the coast on my way to a business meeting with my partner and a new client. Living in Hawaii certainly had its perks (as well as its penalties, such as the cost of living).

I guided my SUV into a narrow parking spot at a casual beachside restaurant on the North Shore of Oahu, and immediately felt overdressed. A group of college-age men strode toward the entrance while an older couple exited arm-in-arm. Not one of these people wore anything beyond board shorts or a summer dress. As I stepped out and smoothed my slacks, I felt envious, wishing I was in board shorts myself.

I met Brian, my business partner, inside. He had cornered a table by the window looking out across a narrow ridge; the ocean was a couple hundred feet away. The place was buzzing and relaxed. I immediately fell into a trance.

Brian told me about Rick, but only in brief. Rick was in his mid-to-late 60s, remarried, and had recently sold a machinery business back in Michigan that he built with his own blood, sweat, and tears. With the $8 million he'd taken away from that deal, he was looking for his next project while attempting to make his money grow.

Waiting for Rick to arrive, Brian was facing away from the entrance, taking full advantage of the view for which Hawaii is famous. I spotted a gorgeous young woman, also overdressed for this particular dining establishment, but she seemed not to care and drew a great deal of attention from the men (and a few women) in the building. I watched her move with a confident swagger, then turn toward the restrooms. Behind her was a man who I would have pegged as her father.

It was Rick. Her husband.

We met and exchanged pleasantries and immediately I sensed a familiar attitude. He was confident, brash, and boastful, and that only increased when his young bride Mimi joined us.

Rick had a happy-hour voice without the need for alcohol. He spoke loud and proud about his life's work and the incredible deal he'd finally made that had turned him from a sometimes-struggling blue-collar business owner into a millionaire.

"Right time, right place," he said about the deal.

Rick was living his dream.

Now he wanted to keep it going, watch it grow, and make sure his new wife was protected after he was gone. He and Mimi had bought a beautiful home on the world-famous Sunset Beach and every day was a vacation for the happy couple.

This couple was a dichotomy. Whereas he strained and struggled, groaned and winced while climbing steps or pulling himself out of his chair, she was lithe and nimble, quick and smooth. Rick was a bit shorter than average and a stiff breeze would have posed trouble for him, whereas she had the height of a model and was quite sharp; it was quickly apparent that she was smarter than he, but she smiled and played the trophy wife part well.

His life story was interesting, to say the least. He dominated the conversation, eager to share his exploits – the near catastrophic conditions that had almost cost him his business, the heroic moves and savvy business decisions that had saved it.

When you have millions in the bank and a dream home on what's considered to be one of the best beaches in the world, it stands to reason you have a bit of bravado.

Listening to him regale us with these stories, knowing what sat in his accounts, I wanted to know his plans for the future. At 67 with that amount of cash, he wouldn't need to do anything else but enjoy life, but the better plan was to invest wisely. Different people have different ideas about what their life should be at that point.

Although initially he stated he wanted to preserve his wealth, what Rick said next was a total contradiction.

Rick said, "I want to trade stocks."

I studied him and noticed a slight smirk from Mimi. She knew something more than I at that time. Rick was convinced that with the Internet taking hold around the world and with so many tech companies exploding in growth, the world wide web was the future of true wealth.

"We don't trade stocks," I told him, "and you won't ever get a call from us about any stock tips."

"Don't need any," he replied, eliciting another facial tic from his wife. I liked this woman immediately. She was charming and funny and reserved. She listened to Rick's tales (probably for the umpteenth time) and did so with a verve I wish I had.

Rick then turned the conversation to us. "Tell me how you guys manage money."

Brian and I laid out our overall strategy. We told Rick about our stock, bond, and commodity allocation and noted that we hired professional money managers for any strategy. When I told him that our *average* returns were in the range of 6-10% over a set course of time based on a variety of risk factors, he scoffed and guffawed.

"I make that in a day!" he said, loud enough for neighboring tables to take notice.

His focus then shifted to learning about our fees and how we conducted our research. He couldn't believe our fees, which were in line with industry standards, and began talking over Brian. "You two couldn't even come close to how much I'm making in just one stock I hold, and you want to charge that?"

I expected Rick to storm off, Mimi in hot pursuit, but he remained. It was then that I saw the other side of Rick, a man who was boastful but had a habit of asking for advice … and wanting it at a much lower price. We call them "askholes."

He wanted to pay bottom-feeder prices for top-tier work.

I wondered how he would have responded if someone had asked him to slash his machinery prices to meet important labor costs but still expected the quality he prod uced. The more we talked over lunch, the more I began to understand him. Part of it was arrogance, but another part was insecurity. Rick was still striving to impress Mimi and talking big was his key language. He had his sights on an even bigger, more grandiose home he wanted to design and have built. I couldn't help but wonder if he felt he needed a bigger home in order to keep Mimi interested.

"If you'd like," I said as the conversation was about to shift to estate planning, my partner's area of expertise, "I'll take a look at your portfolio. For a second opinion," I added for flavor. He agreed.

Brian took over and discussed some steps Rick and Mimi could take to protect her from his children in the future. Rick wasn't very close to his kids for various reasons and he knew there would be a fight over his wealth when he was gone. He wanted to leave them something, but his priority was Mimi. They both listened intently to this advice while I studied Rick's demeanor.

Later that afternoon, I received the information I needed from Rick. Even though he had said he was well diversified, that was far from truthful. Sure, he owned over 30 stocks, but they were all in high tech, and almost all of them were Internet startups. What was also alarming was how much money he put into these. It was staggering.

Digging deeper, I saw that most of these companies didn't produce any revenue and barely registered profits. Even an inexperienced trader would be able to quickly review one of these companies and see it was a risky endeavor, yet millions of people were dumping copious amounts of money into untested companies based on the idea that they would be incredibly profitable simply because they had names ending in *.com*.

Rick owned stock in pets.com and webvan.com, companies that have long since been vanquished. They were just two examples of must-have stocks that "couldn't lose."

Another stock he owned was Dell Computers. Great company, right? Well, back in 1999, this company's stock was soaring so high that if it had continued on that same trajectory, it would be more valuable than the entire U.S. economy! It was clearly unsustainable, but average investors didn't care.

Sustained growth was what so many people were expecting. That's what Rick was expecting. Companies were going public based on nothing more than an idea. It was investment mania and people weren't even thinking twice about it. In fact, it resembled tulip mania all over again.

Tulip mania occurred during the Dutch Golden Age of the early 17th century. Rare versions of the newly introduced tulip bulbs skyrocketed in value because they were suddenly fashionable. Then, in February 1637, the value completely collapsed. Right before the collapse, some tulip bulbs sold for more than 10 times the annual income of a craftsman. Tulip bulbs!

Like Rick, if people had money to invest, they were pouring it into these "tulip bulb" tech companies just because it seemed everyone else was, too. Their advisors were telling them to diversify, to play it smart, to focus on more reasonable returns, but investors were hearing about overnight millionaires and dot-com superheroes; they didn't want slow and steady.

They wanted instantaneous riches.

Rick was right there in the midst of it all. Yes, he was turning some quick, impressive profits – as were many people investing in dot-com companies – but as so many people discovered, profitable stocks mattered only if you got out at the right time. With growth seeming unhindered and explosive, that didn't happen often. Greed took over and Rick became addicted to the rush and enamored with his short-term success, blinding him to the fact that it was due to luck, not skill.

People were quitting their jobs to become full-time traders, even though they had no real experience and knew nothing about it, aside from the "hot ticket" tech companies at that time, and the news media jumped on board, too, making it seem like this new manner of buying and selling stocks (not worrying about revenue, production figures, and other deep insights) was the wave of the future.

It was a time of unprecedented growth in the stock market and Rick was one more shark consuming whatever he could and assuming the ride wouldn't end. He was one more shark who didn't need anyone's advice because, well, frankly, he was *winning*. What could someone like me offer aside from some "safe" ideas that paled in comparison to what was happening in his real life?

Brian and I met with him again, mostly to discuss the estate plan (according to Rick's account of the event). I had taken the information he sent and put together a thorough investment strategy that was sound and diversified. It would provide him steady growth over time and be far less risky than what he was invested in now.

He reviewed it in a matter of seconds, set it aside, and said, "No, thank you. I get everything I need from the newsletters and research reports that come to me." Of course, those newsletters and reports were produced by other dot-com junkies. It would be akin to an alcoholic saying he was fine, that he didn't have a problem while surrounded by his best friends at a local pub.

As a last-ditch effort, I suggested he take a portion of his portfolio and make it safe, meaning setting it aside and protecting it.

"I'll think about it," he answered. His demeanor indicated that wasn't going to happen. He was going to invest, buy, buy, buy, and rake in the millions and, if he were lucky, the tens of millions … all in a matter of months. He had his sights on the new luxurious home he wanted to build.

It was an odd thing, my relationship with Rick. Even though he frustrated me by not taking any of the advice I offered, we stayed in touch. I had no illusions about why. Rick was the type of person who understood the value of my experience, education, and knowledge, even if he wasn't willing to accept any of it at that time.

Six months after our initial meeting, the markets were volatile. Losses were outweighing gains, but like a gambler who'd been pumping big bills into the same slot machine for the past hour or two, with partial wins to keep him locked in place, Rick was rooted. He was staying in … all the way.

In fact, he even doubled down and dropped almost all his remaining cash assets into these tech stocks. It was the Internet, after all; it was the wave of the future and that meant these tech dot-com stocks were *never* going to fail! They couldn't!

He would often say, "John, these stocks were great buys when I bought them, and now they're a steal at these prices"

Mimi was the one who saw the writing on the wall first. She actually started calling Brian and me directly, begging for our help. However, it was Rick's money, and he was able to do whatever he liked with it.

For Rick's part, he was still focused on the research that agreed with him. He certainly saw the articles and reports countering his position and warning people to get out now, but he ignored them. How could he possibly walk away now? Somebody else would be going home with his fortune!

Psychologists have understood this behavior for a long time and it's been labeled the *sunk cost fallacy*. It essentially means someone will stay in a bad situation and expect it to improve, even as all signs indicate otherwise – mostly because they've already invested time (and/or money) into it for a while.

> **Someone will stay in a bad situation and expect it to improve, even as all signs indicate otherwise**

I began to meet with Rick more often, mostly because we had developed a friendship and these past few months were taking a toll on his frame of mind, among other things. He had nearly three-quarters of his life savings tied up in these tech stocks and was beginning to become frantic.

So was the bank that made the loan on his beachfront home. Rick had pledged some of his stock holdings in lieu of a traditional down payment. Why the bank took these stocks as collateral has always confounded me. Now that these stocks had fallen below the bank's comfort level, it was demanding he come up with cash.

A lot of cash.

To add to his misery, he confided that he knew he was losing Mimi, that she was less interested in him, and he was worried about his life's work perishing as the stocks continued their downward trend. Mimi was demanding that he sell, but he was only digging in deeper. I was concerned about him, but just as I thought he might be willing to make some quick changes, he vanished. I kept calling and reaching out but to no avail. Mimi stopped calling as well.

By March 2001, the market had collapsed and eventually I learned that Rick and Mimi had been forced to sell their dream home on the North Shore and move back to the mainland. Rick headed back to Michigan to work for the company he had originally built and sold.

Mimi was never going to move there. She was gone and took half of whatever remained in the divorce.

A life's work perished because Rick refused to listen to sound, reasoned, and experienced advice. He refused to listen to common sense! His insecurities got the best of him, and he allowed his ego to stand front and center in his life and it cost him everything.

He had the world by the tail and tasted the life he dreamed about for decades, but in the end, he believed he knew best.

He didn't need advice.

He became entrenched in the idea that he couldn't lose, that he was making all the right decisions and moves and, like a gambling addict, focused on the wins rather than the losses and didn't know how or when to let go.

> **He didn't "lose it," he let it go.**

I never heard about or from either Rick or Mimi again. It was a tragic tale of having everything and letting it slip away. He didn't "lose it," he let it go. Rick allowed his ego and his arrogance to stand in the way of good decisions and he paid the price.

And no matter how many times we've seen this story unfold in the stock market, very few learn from it.

Trap Three:
Resting in Arrogance

 BELIEFS: I don't need advice. I know what I'm doing. I can outsmart the market.

 EXCUSES: "I know I'm right." "The investment will come back." "What goes down must come back up."

 ACTIONS: Avoiding advice that differs from what you believe to be true.

 RESULTS: Failing to see and acknowledge your weaknesses and losing everything.

Human beings are prideful. You don't have to look far to realize this is true for almost everyone. We take a great deal of pride in how we look, even thinking, "God forbid so-and-so were to see me like this" when just heading out to pick something up from the store late at night.

As we saw in the first story, outward appearance is certainly important to many people and can be their downfall. Constantly thinking things are going to improve, even though the evidence is stacked against that – at least in the short term – can still leave those desperately wanting to convey a certain image digging a deeper and deeper hole.

Pride can cause someone to stay in a particular job too long. People can hang on and hang on and hang on, thinking things are going to improve, that the promotion they've been working toward for so long is finally going to be theirs, completely ignoring the signs that indicate it's going to someone else.

Some people can cling to a particular job or even a career that isn't rewarding in the least, that doesn't provide them any passion or joy, just because of the safety it offers them. If the money is decent, then what's a little aggravation, grief, or feeling as though you're not being fulfilled?

These mistakes often come from a lot of personal issues including insecurity and ego. We can develop a *Belief* system in which we have an almost insatiable need to be right and assume we don't need help. This is all too often rooted in fear.

Some people have a difficult time accepting when they've made a mistake. They hang on to a lie and dig their heels in. Those who have found success can quickly turn away from what helped them rise to their position and forget they didn't do it alone.

This can cause a wide range of other problems, including assuming that since you've made hundreds of thousands or even millions of dollars in your chosen career, perhaps building your own business, you don't need any advice at all.

We saw this in the real estate market in the mid-2000s, as people became real estate gurus overnight when in reality it was mostly luck. You could pick up *The Wall Street Journal,* read a financial book, and take a few online courses, and think you've got it all figured out.

Some people are held captive by their ego, especially when they're chasing an image they believe elevates them even higher in certain social circles. Take Rick in this story.

You don't think he married Mimi for some reason besides her youthful, captivating appearance, do you? He very well might have. She was, after all, funny and highly intelligent.

The two were polar opposites physically, emotionally, and personality-wise, and there is certainly plenty of cynicism among people on the outside looking in, who would say she only married him because of his money. That may have very well been the case, but there could've been something else to it, including an attraction to that confidence that unfortunately bled over into arrogance.

I can only speculate on why Rick was so focused on making sure everyone in the room knew how smart and successful he was. I'm not his psychologist and couldn't tell you what was driving him, but as I worked with numerous clients through the years, I saw arrogance as a defense mechanism.

Many of the most arrogant people you will ever meet are either:

a) Incredibly intelligent, successful people who believe they've earned the right to be arrogant

b) Insecure

I pegged Rick as the latter. He built up a series of *Excuses* for why he carried himself the way he did. He relied on his financial success but constantly worried about how people (including his own family) would see him.

If I'm right, his insecurity is what drove him to seek out a younger wife, the beachfront luxury home, and the fancy sports car. His *Actions* were rooted in his need to be viewed as intelligent to compensate for his appearance, successful to make up for his stature, cool for his aging body. He was looking to feel youthful again, especially as doubts may have begun pervading his thoughts. When you face your own mortality, whether it's in your teens, 20s, 40s, 60s, or 70s, it can be unsettling.

GETTING CAUGHT

Beliefs: I don't need advice. I know what I'm doing. I can outsmart the market. Rick wanted everyone to think he was the smartest person in the room. We may read a number of books, check out some blogs online, and become too comfortable in the (limited) knowledge we gain; when that happens, it creates a self-perpetuating system whereby we gain more attention, are sought after, and begin to build a false narrative around our lives.

Excuses: "I know I'm right." "The investment will come back." "What goes down must come back up." Thanks to the Internet, we have access to so much information, it's mind-boggling. This access can make some people appear as though they know everything (or at least a lot), when in fact their knowledge base is faulty.

 Actions: Avoiding advice that differs from what you believe to be true. We tend to dismiss advice that counters what we know, because our belief system is rooted in the need to be right. The fact that this information comes from credible and reliable sources means nothing, so long as we can cling to our ideas.

 Results: Failing to see and acknowledge your weaknesses and losing everything. When our beliefs are so mired in a need to be right about everything, we can quickly slip down a slippery slope leading to ruin. Since this belief is rooted deep within our psyche, we're willing to put everything we have on the line to prove we're smart, savvy, and right.

They say arrogance requires advertising and confidence speaks for itself. In the business world, confidence is essential, but arrogance will sabotage you. If you don't have confidence, you will thoroughly get chewed up and spit out in most business environments. If you're driven by arrogance, you will most certainly suffer, but in a subtler manner.

> **They say arrogance requires advertising and confidence speaks for itself. In the business world, confidence is essential, but arrogance will sabotage you.**

Suppliers, competitors, and even employees can all test your resolve and if you build a successful business over time, you will develop that same type of confidence. Unfortunately, if you don't control it, it can lead you into a new set of beliefs. It's those beliefs that can cause you to fall over into arrogance and get trapped there.

Rick simply didn't want to appear unknowledgeable. Not in front of his wife. As I mentioned, she was quite intelligent herself, so he might've already been insecure before they met; then, captivated by her beauty and youth, he had no intention of letting her get away. However, her intelligence may have been threatening to him, so he focused on *seeming* smarter than everyone else, even though he wasn't.

When you rest in arrogance, when you assume you can figure everything out on your own and need no advice or counsel, you've got a serious problem. Even leaders in industry, medicine, and government rely on others for advice because they understand they can't possibly know everything or be an expert at everything. Similarly, top athletes rely heavily on their coaches – a pro golfer may engage a swing coach, long drive coach, a sports psychologist, personal trainer, physiotherapist, and more.

Rick was going to do whatever he wanted with his money. No one could tell him otherwise, not even highly trained and experienced financial advisors and consultants. He was focused on hitting the jackpot to fulfill his ego rather than taking the slow, methodical, more prudent path to grow his wealth.

The *Results* were that he ultimately lost everything, including his new wife. To make matters worse, I later found out that he had to return to the company he'd sold and work as an employee during the time of his life when he should have been out enjoying it, living on the beach and traveling the world.

A belief system that is rooted in your perceived intelligence, that your assumptions are correct and that you alone can figure things out, is a dangerous platform upon which to stand. As things begin crumbling, you won't be looking outward for help; you'll continue to look inward and every time, unless you're exceedingly lucky at the very right moment, you will lose.

Robert Kiyosaki often tells me how important it is to rely on others. He says, "Life is a team sport and if we try to go it alone, we'll run into some major hurdles along the way."

He and his wife, Kim, have built amazing wealth and success, but they rely on advisors and their support network more and more. It's good counsel.

The next time you hear somebody say, "I don't need any advice," *pay attention.* What kind of advice are they turning away? Is it something they truly have experience with, such as within their career? Is it something they certainly aren't an expert in? Or is it something within themselves they're vigorously trying to hide?

> **"Life is a team sport and if we try to go it alone, we'll run into some major hurdles along the way."**

Pay attention to what happens in the aftermath. What if things don't work out for them? Do they fall? Were they devastated or hurt? We don't want to rejoice in anyone's failure, no matter how much money they may have earned or inherited; rather, pay attention to how much ego and arrogance played a role in their downfall.

Remember, you don't know it all, no matter what schools you went to or what degrees you have or where you work or what you read every day. In fact, the more you have of that "stuff," the more likely you may overlook things, approach things with biases, misguide yourself, allow your ego to guide you, and in the end miss huge opportunities.

When that happens, you're more likely to ignore good advice. There's no reason to look back and remember somebody gave you sound advice and you let it slip away.

YOUR TURN

Let's take another look at your life. Keep things in perspective. Pull out your guidebook and complete Activity #6.

This is another opportunity to begin diving deep down to the roots and see how your beliefs are impacting your financial life.

CHAPTER 9

Reason Four:
It's Too Late

It's a typical morning. You wake up at the usual time, stretch, and crawl out of bed. Or perhaps you're a morning person and leap out from under the covers, ready to tackle the day. The morning sun is just beginning to paint colors along the distant skyline, promising a beautiful day.

You stroll to the kitchen and grab a cup of steaming coffee (already brewed thanks to the high-tech pot with an exceptional timer) and the paper is delivered perfectly just outside your front door. In your robe and slippers you nestle into a lounge chair and read the news.

After a long, hot shower and dressing in your normal business attire, you're heading through rush hour traffic to work. You decide to stop along the way for a bagel and a quick lottery ticket. Waiting in line, you pull out your debit card. Once the total is rung up, you insert the card, jab the numbers for your PIN, and wait for the familiar warning tone to remind you to take your card back.

"Denied," the attendant says with no emotion in his voice.

Your brow furrows and you tell him to run it again.

He does as instructed, then shakes his head.

"You have cash?" he asks.

No. You don't. Most of the time you're simply swiping credit or debit cards these days. Something's not right, but you want to grab this stuff and go, so you take out the credit card.

"Lottery is debit only," the attendant says.

By now you're getting frustrated and taking it out on him. You tell him to forget the scratch offs, vowing to never set foot in this quickie mart ever again, and swipe your credit card.

It, too, is denied.

You hurry out of the store as quickly as possible, feeling the burning and judgmental glare of the worker and everyone else in line behind you. *He doesn't even have credit!* They say to themselves, or so you assume.

Feeling flustered, you open your banking app on your smartphone to check your balance. It's overdrawn. You can't figure it out. There should have been thousands in the checking and another $20k in reserve checking, not to mention the $65k in savings.

Checking is overdrawn and the other accounts have nothing in them. The more you dig into things, the worse it gets. Your mortgage is at the max, there are credit cards in your name you knew nothing about, and the IRS claims you haven't paid on your outstanding tax balance in years.

Essentially, you're beyond broke … you're bankrupt. Why? Because the person you trusted with your finances committed fraud. This person is not your financial advisor. This person is your spouse.

This isn't a fairy tale or one of Aesop's Fable; this is reality for far too many people who relied on their spouse or partner, who trusted their husband or wife or partner in life with everything, never asking the right questions and never getting involved in their financial life in any way, shape, or form.

My close friend Kim Kiyosaki often talks about and quotes in her book that I highly recommend, *Rich Woman: Take Charge of Your Money. Take Charge of Your Life*, some startling statistics: Women are far more likely to become widowed than men and fully one-third who are widowed have that dubious distinction before they reach 60. In fact, half of all women who are widowed are 65 or *younger*. And according to the stats, they can expect to live another 20 years at least, on average.

Alone.

Of the elderly living in poverty, three out of four are women. 7 out of 10 women will live in poverty at some time in their life. 90% of all women will have the sole responsibility of finances in their lifetime ... 79% of all women have not planned for this. 80% of widowed women living in poverty were *not* poor while their husbands were alive.

Of the elderly living in poverty, three out of four are women.

Please take a moment and let those numbers sink in.

These stats *do not* imply women are incapable of managing finances; in fact, in my experience many of them are far *more* capable ... it's that they were deceived or trusted their husbands too much with the finances in their marriage. They didn't want to interfere.

Such was the case for Dottie.

I established my reputation as a solid financial planner with a strong knowledge of estate and trust planning, and eventually attorneys were referring people to me more and more. They typically brought me in to sort through and organize finances that in most cases were a mess – statements, policies, documents, and tax returns scattered all throughout the house.

Unfortunately, most of the time I'd be called in too late, after the damage had been done. I was not so much a planner for these individuals as a cleanup specialist, someone who sorted out the estate and organized the financial picture for the surviving spouse. I earned a specialized certification in this area because of this growing trend and began acting as both a financial consultant and a consoling force in a devastated life.

I moved back to L.A. in 2013 to focus on my new financial transformation program, with a mission to transform the world's relationship with money. That's when a former high school friend reached out to me. He heard I was living in the area and his aunt was in dire straits.

Dottie and Jack had been married for 42 years. They had four children. They'd lived a good life, for all intents and purposes. He owned nice cars, always had to have a high-end watch strapped around his wrist, and talked big about many of his past adventures, dealings, and offers.

He did what he could to help his children, giving them money or buying them things whenever it seemed they were in another bind (which was often, even as they moved through their 20s and into their 30s).

When he was 68, Jack suffered a stroke. It left him comatose for several weeks, and for the next year and a half, he was essentially bedridden, unable to move about without considerable help and a wheelchair. Dottie was his primary caregiver, though they had aides and visiting nurses helping every week.

Before the stroke, Dottie and Jack had a joint checking account, and despite their expenses and him no longer employed full-time, that account continued to increase; she had no reason not to believe his boasts about successful business ventures, consulting jobs, investments, and so on. She was seeing their money *grow!*

Toward the end, Jack was moved to a nursing home, which they had to pay for themselves. There was a life insurance policy on Jack in the amount of $1 million, of which Dottie was the sole beneficiary. Despite all the heartache and pain they were enduring with his health deteriorating, Dottie was at peace. She felt confident she wouldn't need to worry about money the rest of her life. She believed she was financially set.

Jack's health continued to decline and finally in December, just before Christmas, he passed away. Dottie was both sad and relieved; she'd been taking care of him for so long, expending every ounce of her energy to support him, that she had given up every other aspect of her life. She also knew it was time. Jack's quality of life had diminished to the point that he wasn't able to do much of anything.

Jack and Dottie had inherited their home from his parents many years earlier, and given its location, it was valued at over $1 million. It was certainly more than Dottie would need, with the children out of the house. The house was another asset she could count on, if needed.

The funeral was smaller than she would have expected, considering how many people Jack knew and how many business dealings he'd had through the years. Two of their children "couldn't make it" to the service and that really upset Dottie. Despite their absence, they would return for something far more important to them then their father.

After nearly two years of taking care of Jack, she desperately needed a break. A close friend agreed to look after the house while she was away, and she headed out with no return date in mind. She decided to fulfill that dream she and Jack had talked about for many years which was renting a house on the coast for several months. She had over $200,000 in the checking account, so there was no hurry.

While Dottie was away, her friend would call from the house with increasing frequency. Two of her kids had stopped by and "tried to gain access to their father's study," but Dottie's friend wouldn't permit it. A couple of other individuals had been by on more than a few occasions. They were asking for Jack and claiming he owed them "some money." When they were told he passed away, they simply walked off, never asking about his wife or their property or any next of kin. They would later return.

After three months away, Dottie figured it was time to return home and deal with the estate and other necessities. As Dottie began settling into this new life as a widow, her friend's reports didn't really worry her. She recalled Jack's promises and his stories of military experience and professional life … he'd shared all of it with the goal of impressing others and making his wife happy and comfortable, without the burden of financial stress.

She never questioned any of it.

Ten days later, I entered Dottie's world. I got her call in the morning and it was a familiar refrain.

"I'm in trouble. Can you help?"

I arrived at Dottie's house soon after and I saw her demeanor fall hour by hour. Even though she'd had suspicions that things weren't quite what they'd seemed before Jack passed away, nothing had prepared her for the reality.

Jack essentially lied about everything.

He hadn't been a savvy businessman. He hadn't consulted for companies or offered advice on how they could improve production or sales or revenue. In fact, Dottie struggled to find one small thing relating to their finances that Jack had been honest about. She could only find it in their joint checking account, which now held just under $165,000 after her vacation and other expenses.

The life insurance policy Dottie was expecting (and I'd have to say counting on) wasn't in place; Jack stopped paying on it a couple years earlier. The people who had stopped by looking for Jack were part of a, shall we say, "private" lender, and they were going to collect.

When Jack retired, he had taken a full pension but hadn't opted in for the spousal beneficiary option, which meant Dottie would no longer receive anything from that fund. As for the house, he had borrowed so heavily against it that she was now underwater – on a million-dollar property.

By lunchtime, neither of us had an appetite. We skipped lunch so we could finish this up and move on to the next step: trying to make sense of where Dottie could go from here.

Jack had taken out numerous credit cards when things were going well enough and paid off one with the other. He'd continued to play this far-too-common shell game until his stroke. Now Dottie was sacked with over $100,000 in these debts on top of everything else. I couldn't tell her what would happen with the "private" lender; I didn't have experience dealing with loan sharks and the like, nor do I ever want to. We found a lawyer for that nightmare.

She was forced to sell the house and she lost the cars and much of her property and possessions due to liquidation of assets. With another savings account, she managed to hold onto that money, which eventually topped out at just shy of $220,000, but I had no illusions that was going to last long – not because of her lifestyle but rather her children.

Jack had been so focused on being liked that he had given his children whatever they asked for. As Dottie soon learned, none of the four was financially independent. They'd all been tapping into their father's generosity for most of their post-college days and were now bitter that the gravy train was over. They blamed Dottie, claiming she was either lying or had ruined their father financially.

She failed to recognize the warning signs that had been building for the previous five or ten years. She and Jack hadn't gone out with friends. She'd rarely ever met people who had worked with, for, or had business relationships with her husband anymore. She noticed he was becoming more and more distant, but she simply wrote it off as having been together for so long that they'd needed their own space. Given that they were no longer receiving financial support, two of her own children simply didn't call or visit anymore. To Dottie, that didn't make sense, and although she was hurt, she didn't want to push the issue with them.

Jack left no will and there was no family trust. He hadn't worked in years. Unbelievably disgraceful, their children would soon be threatening a lawsuit claiming what they believed to be their entitled share of the inheritance. Of course, this was ridiculous as there were no legal grounds for such a threat, but it certainly didn't help the situation. Soon after, her children turned against each other and a family battle raged. Regardless of my support and that of her attorney, Dottie felt the huge strain wear on her as she became more and more vulnerable. This psychological nightmare was having an impact on her physical and emotional life. No amount of consoling would help her feel better about things. She lost everything including the one thing she thought she could count on, her family.

I stayed in touch with her for a while, but our contact slowly dissipated. In the end, I think our phone calls and visits were just too painful for both of us. Our personal interactions were merely a reminder of the tragedy she had endured.

Where she had been with Jack, the life they had been living, I can only imagine the struggle she faced in the next several years trying to adjust and find a way to bring in more income for the rest of her life. At 67 years old, Dottie had to start over again

Dottie grew up in a generation where husbands and wives had specific roles to fulfill and it was her understanding that finances were his domain. She never thought to question him.

My grandparents were a great example of a solid relationship where both individuals had specific roles to play, but each understood everything about their finances. It's an important lesson we should all keep in mind, especially as we move toward retirement and especially if the relationship cools or new 'behaviors' begin taking root.

> **Sometimes we just don't want to see those warning signs.**

Dottie missed the signs and while tragic, it wasn't without warning. Sometimes we just don't want to see those warning signs.

Trap Four:
In the Wake ...

 BELIEFS: My spouse handles the finances in the family.

 EXCUSES: "He/she knows what they're doing so there's no need for me to get involved."

 ACTIONS: Putting all your faith in your spouse. Not asking questions, looking for signs, or dealing with the stress of financial health and well-being.

 RESULTS: Waking up one day, alone, only to discover your Golden Years lack the gold you anticipated.

Losing someone you love can cause tremendous grief. In the wake of that loss, we can become lost ourselves, at least for a while.

Too often people can become intimidated in relationships and even marriages to the point where they're afraid to even discuss the household finances and what will happen financially if someone dies. They just assume everything's fine, trusting their spouse with the details they don't know much about, don't really care about, or don't think are important.

Having this *Belief* that everything is as it seems but not having a clue where all the financial resources happen to be is a dangerous situation. For Dottie, she was confident in the fact that everything was in order, even well after Jack suffered his stroke. The affairs of her husband were his business, according to her mode of thinking. He was going to take care of her and there was no reason he would ever lie about their financial situation.

For her, the marriage had been good, she had been a loyal and faithful wife, and he had provided fairly well most of their life together, so what reason would she have to doubt him?

She built into her mindset a series of *Excuses* that since everything seemed to be fine, they were.

What I noticed growing up, working on my grandparents' farm every other summer, was that my grandmother knew every detail of their finances, same as my grandfather. They had no secrets. That went for my parents, too, who had the same policy of transparency.

Dottie and Jack took the opposite approach. But the more I dug in, the more I began to realize that it wasn't so much that Dottie wasn't interested but rather that Jack was evasive.

Dottie admitted that during the early part of their marriage, she tried to become involved, to understand finances, to know where the money was coming in and where it was going out, but Jack resisted her at almost every turn. That led her to simply give up.

She learned far too late that some things are worth the fight.

But marriages are unions of two independent individuals coming together. The couple will share not only a house and a bed but every aspect of their lives; they should be working together for their future.

There are numerous reasons people try to hide certain facets of their financial circumstances from their spouses. It may be that they've fallen behind, they're embarrassed, or they simply don't want to deal with the stress that uncomfortable conversations and arguments could have in their lives.

Modern working environments, whether on a farm or in corporate America, can be exceedingly stressful – physically, emotionally, and mentally draining. The last thing people want to deal with when they return home is more anxiety.

Instead of taking *Action* and confronting the situation, they hide their money problems. They may even take some money out of their savings and invest it in what they deem to be a worthy stock or other option only to find out later on they were fooled or made a bad decision. Instead of confronting the issue and being honest, they double down.

And just like somebody with an addiction, they do whatever they can to hide the truth from the people who love them the most.

They don't want to be judged. They don't want to be ridiculed. They don't want to be embarrassed. Most importantly to them, though, they don't want to be forced to stop.

Infidelity is nothing new. It's been around for as long as the institution of marriage. While devastating enough to end many marriages, it's not the only kind of cheating that takes place.

Any time a spouse (or partner in a long-term relationship, for that matter) carries on a continuing lie, that's cheating. It's being unfaithful to someone they claim to love. Ultimately, it doesn't matter if the lie seemed like a small thing at the time – it can do tremendous damage.

One spouse may be abused – financially, emotionally, and/or physically – which causes them to be afraid to even ask questions. Others simply put their trust in their spouse, thinking everything will work out based on what's being said, but they never verify any of it.

In the end, I discovered through my former high school classmate, that Dottie managed to escape with something in her bank account. She had Social Security and a small pension from an earlier short-lived teaching job, which provided an opportunity to start over. She would get by even if that meant getting a job and finding a way to navigate the future. Many women don't have that opportunity. They wake up one morning thinking everything's fine only to realize they're beyond broke; they're bankrupt and still legally and financially responsible for a host of debts.

> **80% of widowed women living in poverty were *not* poor while their husbands were alive.**

Remember what I said earlier: 80% of widowed women living in poverty were ***not*** poor while their husbands were alive.

It doesn't have to be too late for anyone. Spouses need to take charge and realize this is their life that's on the line, too.

GETTING CAUGHT

Beliefs: My spouse handles the finances in the family. Whether by tradition, culture, or simply a desire not to have to deal with financial concerns, putting your future in the hands of your partner in this life may seem noble, but you need to ask yourself if it's rooted in something more and whether or not things are as you were told they are.

Excuses: "He/she knows what they're doing so there's no need for me to get involved." As long as the outward appearance of one's financial life seems good enough, then it's easy to make excuses to not ask questions, especially if questions create tension within the relationship.

Actions: Putting all your faith in your spouse. Not asking questions, looking for signs, or dealing with the stress of financial health and well-being. It's important that each of us keep our eyes open and pay attention to subtle signs that may indicate not everything is as good as it appears.

Results: Waking up one day, alone, only to discover your Golden Years may lack the gold you anticipated. No one wants to wake up one day, widowed and alone, and realize they don't have nearly the money they thought they had waiting for them. That is no way to finish out what some consider to be the best years of our lives.

When it comes to financial freedom and peace of mind, everyone involved must be ***involved***.

If Dottie had asserted her authority, demanded her respect as part of this legal and spiritual union in marriage, if she had stepped up and pressured her husband to be forthright and honest with their financial situation, to take a look at the bank statements, the bills, the credit card debts, and everything else, the *Results* could have been different. She may have seen something far earlier than she did.

This belief that everything's fine, even in the face of activities that don't make sense, is dangerous. Her excuse was that she trusted her husband, but even more than that, she simply didn't have the strength to fight.

It's hard to blame Dottie. That's how she was raised and that's what she was taught. Rather than lay blame, the important thing to do is make sure you're involved in the financial decisions of your household. It's vitally important to schedule some time at least once a month to review the financial affairs. Trust and respect are wonderful things, but it's a street that runs in both directions.

> **Make sure you're involved in the financial decisions of your household**

The more engaged you are in the finances, the more you'll **help** your spouse or partner through even the most difficult circumstances. Please, don't be a member of the 80% club. You deserve so much more.

YOUR TURN

Let's take another look at your life. Keep things in perspective. Pull out your guidebook and complete Activity #7.

This is another opportunity to begin diving deep down to the roots and see how your beliefs are impacting your financial life.

CHAPTER 10

Reason Five:
I Don't Have Time

Years ago, Ashley dated Dan, one of the guys I played rugby with. She was a vibrant, energetic woman with great plans for her life. I spent a bit of time at her apartment with Dan and a few others, and we talked often about our experiences, our hopes, and our ambitions.

She and Dan didn't last all that long, though they parted amicably enough. Like so many who drift in and slip away, she faded into the tapestry of my past.

Many years later, I ran into her. I was shocked to learn she married a notorious local attorney in Southern California. Her husband, Harvey, was the kind of man you hope to never cross paths with in legal circles, never sit opposite in court, and never inadvertently invite to a party at your house. He was at least 20 years older, unhealthy looking and a slob in every sense of the word – physically, verbally, and emotionally. If ever there was a man I would say I never want my daughter to date, much less marry, that would be him.

I was surprised, to say the least. Ashley had never impressed me as someone who would settle down with a man so openly and obviously different on almost every level. But Ashley had two young boys. She struggled for a long time to raise them and scrounge together enough money to survive, so I could at least understand her motivation. In marrying Harvey, she'd been able to quit her teaching job to stay home with her kids. I'd heard that Harvey was so successful as a plaintiff's attorney that he was quite well off financially. The trappings of materialism, not having to worry about money anymore – especially if you're struggling to raise a young family on your own – can be a powerful force.

Apparently, Harvey also knew about me because as our worlds collided in the international aisle at a local grocery, he said, "Oh, yeah, the financial guy." He glanced at Ashley and said, "You hooked up with one of his rugby pals, right?"

It was unnerving. It's not like I was world-renowned in my field, but apparently she had mentioned her past to Harvey, and somehow my name got rolled in.

My friend Dan later confided to me that Harvey had been in a long-term marriage that had recently ended. He had full-grown children, but the rumor around town was that he cheated on his wife and things didn't end well. Not exactly the model of character one might pursue for their own spouse, but for some reason Ashley and Harvey hit it off. They'd ended up living in a very upscale neighborhood.

Ashley appeared to have grown comfortable with this new life. She even admitted (though a bit sheepishly at first), "Life is good." I didn't really believe her. There was something else there, some sense of doubt, sadness, or worry in her voice.

In essence, Ashley married for safety and security. Harvey married in some effort to capture lost youth and found it in her. I couldn't help but think that neither of them married for love.

As they began to build their life together, Ashley was taking a greater interest in their financial future. She told Harvey after he returned from a business trip that she wanted the two of them to come and visit me. He wasn't interested. She was persistent. She told me on the phone, "I'm going to get him in to see you."

To be honest, I wasn't interested, either. I didn't want to work with this man, but I liked Ashley. I respected her. We had been friends once, and I was concerned about her and her future. If there was some way I could help, I would.

Surprisingly, Harvey showed up with her at my office at our scheduled time. He was crass, foul-mouthed, and condescending. I could tell immediately he needed to be the smartest person in the room, and that was fine with me. I'd just let him talk.

He didn't seem interested in being there. In fact, his cell phone rang more than a few times, and he took the calls as I was sitting behind my desk trying to explain a few things to him and Ashley. His phone would ring and he'd dig it out of his pocket, making a big scene about the whole thing, look at the screen, and either smirk and shove it back in his pocket while it continued to blare. Or he'd stab the green answer button and yammer away as loudly as he could.

Ashley was polite and gracious, apologizing profusely every time he took a call. She seemed genuinely embarrassed by his behavior, but then again anyone who knew him would expect such things from him.

Eventually we got around to talking about their financial situation. As I had heard, he was recently divorced, having been married for over 30 years. His adult children and he were estranged. In fact, any time the topic of his children came up, he would kind of roll his eyes and snicker.

He seemed oblivious to the emotional pain that someone in his situation would feel. I got the sense from his bravado that he was hurting over the situation. However, showing weakness as a plaintiff's attorney was a dangerous thing, and many attorneys will carry a false exterior even into their family lives.

Harvey complained about the divorce proceedings, claiming he'd gotten ripped off. I found it interesting that he was this high-profile plaintiff's attorney and someone had managed to get the best of him in court. I had to remind myself that divorce attorneys are different from plaintiff's attorneys; they practice a different type of law, and there are many moving parts in these proceedings.

There was an underlying resentment, even an anger brewing beneath the surface when the topic of his divorce or first marriage came up. He married Ashley shortly after the divorce was finalized and, as so many are apt to realize, that's not always the best starting point.

As we finally dug into their financial situation, it became clear that Harvey was not as wealthy as he appeared. It was another case of putting on a false front. In his legal circles there was an image to uphold, an idea other lawyers and his clients needed to have about him.

How could he impress clients wearing a low-priced suit from a local department store? He had to have the best of the best: the Italian suits, the $500 shoes, and the $2,000 Rolex watch. And let's not forget the Mercedes-Benz.

However, he was highly leveraged in debt. He was still paying off the court settlement from the divorce proceedings in order to even things out between him and his ex-wife. He flat-out refused to let go of the house. That had been one of many major contentious points in the divorce proceedings, as his wife had fought diligently for it.

It was one of his few victories, one he was extremely proud of, even though he'd been ordered to pay his ex-wife half the value of the house. I'm not exactly sure of the divorce settlement details, but from what I gathered, that house was listed at over $1.5 million. After factoring in the mortgage and some negotiations with the attorneys, that meant he had to come up with $500,000 for her on top of the other assets he had to split. He was going to be paying that debt for a long time on top of alimony, which turned out to be a hefty sum.

He brushed all this off, saying, "My entire focus now is on my practice. We got some great cases in the pipeline. Things will be fine."

I looked to Ashley when he said this, but I didn't get a sense she was disappointed he was putting his work ahead of his spouse. *Maybe this is different,* I thought. Maybe they truly did love one another and there was an understanding about expectations they had right from the start.

After dealing with 50 minutes of his phone calls, his account of the battle scars from his divorce, and his boasts about the success he was finding with his new practice, I was able to tease out their main reason for visiting me.

It had to do with paperwork.

Ashley wanted to make sure the estate-planning paperwork was all in order. She was smart enough to see the warning signs already. She also understood that his high-stress job and a number of bad habits were affecting his health, even though he refused to acknowledge any of it.

The main focus was the beneficiary designation changes for his 401(k) and life insurance policy. Harvey didn't seem all that concerned, but Ashley wasn't sure how everything stood. At that moment, Harvey had a $1.5-million life insurance policy and after the divorce settlement, $700,000 in retirement accounts. Those were some impressive numbers, and that meant digging through the documentation carefully in order to make sure everything was as it should be for their new life together.

I told them that the sooner they got all this worked out, the better. "You never know what can happen," I said.

I mentioned they needed to get the proper forms from their 401(k) provider and life insurance company. This was usual stuff, but in my experience the usual stuff is also the kind of stuff people tend to put off. The other problem I often see that causes so many financial headaches, problems, and disasters is that no one keeps track or properly organizes their documents. As simple as that sounds, it's a leading cause of so many financial failures.

> **In my experience the usual stuff is also the kind of stuff people tend to put off**

I also discussed his overall portfolio and long-term planning. Harvey wasn't interested. He pressed forth with his belligerent attitude, claiming he knew what he was doing and didn't need my help.

There were a few follow-up phone calls between me and Ashley and every time I asked about the forms, she would just say, "I don't want to bother him right now. He's so busy traveling, with court cases, and all that other stuff. He says he just doesn't have the time yet. But he will."

Once again, the unpredictable strikes hard and things were about to take a horrible turn for the worse.

About eight months after that meeting in my office, Ashley called again. There was something in her voice that immediately told of trouble. I thought, *Oh no, he's divorcing her*. She still had young boys to take care of, and if they weren't diligent in getting the paperwork sorted out, she might be back to square one.

"John," she said to me, "Harvey is dead."

I was stunned. I didn't know what to say.

She went on. "Well, he's in a coma, but the doctors say he's not going to make it."

I have to admit, my first thought was the paperwork – did he get it completed? The next thing she said confirmed my biggest concern. None of the beneficiary paperwork had been filled out or signed. I sat at my desk, phone pressed to my ear and my forehead against my free hand. I knew Ashley was in big financial trouble.

I gave her the number of two attorneys and told her she needed to get legal counsel. She needed to do this immediately because a man in a coma cannot sign legal documents. This was going to be a serious problem for her.

There was no recourse with the shared property because it was now almost fully leveraged in debt. And based on what the beneficiary documents stated, she wasn't going to get anything because Harvey's ex-wife Nancy was first in line.

Two days later, Harvey passed away. The day after that I met with Ashley. Next to my initial meeting with Dottie from the previous story, that was arguably the second worst meeting I've ever had. She wept profusely for the longest time, and I felt awkward, incapable of offering any real consolation.

She had so many regrets and even more fear. She admitted that Harvey had been her ticket to financial security for her and her two young boys. Now she was going to be starting all over, possibly in worse shape than when she had met him.

Fortunately, after we went through all the financial documentation, I saw that she was going to walk away with about $100,000. In my experience, especially when people grow accustomed to the good life, that doesn't last long.

Toward the end of our conversation, Ashley looked up at me through red, puffy eyes, and asked, "Will you speak to Nancy?"

First, I had never met Nancy, knew nothing about her, and frankly had no desire to go down that road. After all, Nancy had been married to this man for over 30 years, had raised children with him, and there were bound to be strong emotional reactions to his passing. Second, given what Nancy had to endure for so many years, I was confident in her answer.

I recommended having her attorney contact Nancy, but as we discussed it further, we both realized that might come across as threatening. In the end, I agreed to make the call.

Beneficiary designations supersede what may be expressed in a will. Even if Harvey had changed his will, his ex-wife Nancy would still inherit certain assets if they hadn't been changed in the beneficiary designations, as these are legal documents.

Ashley understood that taking legal action in this type of case was a longshot at best and would be incredibly costly. Whatever money she could walk away with would likely be eaten up in legal fees.

When I was finally alone, I made the phone call. Nancy was extremely nice, and it surprised me. Despite his infidelity, she seemed genuinely sad that Harvey was gone. She also expressed sympathy for Ashley. I got the sense she viewed Ashley as a vulnerable young woman and somebody who was naïve and had gotten suckered into life with Harvey. After all, Nancy lived with him for 30 years and knew him quite well.

However, Nancy was also honest and stated she wanted payback. She had left college and her career to raise their kids. Divorced at 60 plus years old, her once stable life was now filled with uncertainty and her long-term financial security was in doubt. With Harvey gone, her alimony payments had stopped. On top of all that, she had two children and future grandchildren who she wanted to leave an inheritance to when she passed away.

After a week passed and Nancy had a chance to reflect on the situation, she explained to me that it was her faith and her empathy for Ashley and those two young boys that changed her mind. In the end, she felt compelled to share in some of the assets Harvey left behind. All told, Ashley walked away with the amount held in one of his IRA accounts.

Ashley got lucky and walked away with enough money to support her and her kids while she got back on her feet, but it could have been much different.

Ashley knew proper paperwork and legal filings were important, but she didn't want to make waves or push Harvey too hard. I guess it may have felt to her like greed constantly talking about those issues, but she learned that you never know when your time – or the time of a loved one – will be up.

When you have important documents to fill out and file, do it right away. There's no reason to delay. You have the time.

When you have important documents to fill out and file, do it right away. There's no reason to delay. You have the time.

Trap Five:
Who Needs Tomorrow?

 BELIEFS: I don't have time now, but I can always get to it later.

 EXCUSES: "Life is just too busy right now."

 ACTIONS: Procrastinating.

 RESULTS: Tragedy can strike at any time.

How many times have you said to yourself or someone else, *"I just don't have time"?* Even though we have the best of everything, technological advancements that would make our grandparents blush, especially for just how much time it saves us from everyday tasks, we never seem to have time for important things.

What was the last thing you put off because you "simply didn't have time"? I want you to take a moment right now and think about that.

Was it the documents your accountant requested? Was it filling out some paperwork for your child's education? How about calling AT&T about that $50 overcharge on last month's cell phone bill? Was it making a phone call to a parent, sibling, or friend you haven't spoken to in years? What about your living will you keep putting off?

Was it something for work?

Ultimately, it doesn't matter what it was; the point here is that we make excuses to avoid doing a long list of things we should take care of immediately. We develop a *Belief* that you don't have time now, but there will be time later.

IT'S NOT A PRIORITY

What I want you to do instead of accepting those *Excuses* is to change them. Instead of saying, "I don't have time," say to yourself, "It's not a priority."

Now see how things line up.

Suddenly everything comes into focus, doesn't it? Not purchasing a life insurance policy when you have young children and a spouse relying on you – could certainly be brushed off if you don't think you have time to deal with it. But in reality, how long is it going to take you to search for and choose a simple insurance policy? 30 minutes? 15?

Getting a life insurance policy is an important aspect of being a responsible adult with a family. When you say you don't have time to pursue it, look into it, or purchase one, what are you really saying?

It's not a priority.

"But John," you may be arguing, "I really *don't* have time."

I would have you analyze your situation and ask yourself what you did last night. When you got home from work, did you just eat, spend a few moments with your children, and then go to bed, being fast asleep within 10 minutes? I highly doubt that.

Many people will sit around talking, watching a television program to relax, sipping on wine or a cold beer, texting a friend, spending time on the computer, or making a few phone calls to catch up with others. Those are all fine things to do, but when you say you don't have time, it really means what you're avoiding is simply not a priority.

And what does that really mean?

There are people out there who are incredibly busy, working two or three jobs, raising children as a single parent, and struggling just to keep up with the regular housework and preparing meals. Those are the people who could truly say they don't have time for other things, but I bet they could scrape together an hour or two every few days to take care of high-priority issues.

Most people put in a 40-hour work week. Add in their commute and let's call it 50 hours. Did you realize there are 168 hours in a week? I think you know where I'm going here. Everyone can find time to get important things done. It boils down to priority.

In this story, Ashley's *Actions* involved putting off the most important aspect of documentation and paperwork in her marriage. She had the incorrect belief that there was always going to be another opportunity, another tomorrow.

Sure, there is. Until it's gone.

You may say in Ashley's defense that she was dealing with a rude, stubborn, and obnoxious mule who made these types of things difficult. Frankly this is just another excuse. Frankly I'm tired of hearing this because all it does is lead to more stress, pain, and problems. For those of you reading this who are in a similar situation as Ashley, you have no other choice than to take firm action – whatever that may be – to get these things accomplished. Otherwise, you're setting yourself up for failure.

I've seen this story unfold far too many times.

The *Action* is that we do nothing, and the unexpected comes before we're ready.

Some people make excuses and procrastinate because they don't want to confront their own mortality. Some procrastinate because they honestly don't think the issue is all that important. Some people procrastinate because they don't want to deal with boring stuff.

Whatever the cause, it leads to a pattern, and it's usually not isolated. We can look at Harvey's life and speculate that he was a man who likely took very little interest in his long-term plans. He may have always been that way, chasing the current case and surrounding himself in the comforts that mattered most to him at the time. Maybe he only invested in a 401(k) or life insurance policy because of the persistence of his first wife, and his retirement account was set up for him by his company.

We can surmise these things but can't know for sure. However, the story isn't really about Harvey; it's about us.

We become adept at making excuses for putting things off. When we have someone facilitating those excuses, enabling us to continue doing that, it just expands the cycle, putting off the most important decisions, paperwork, and corrections that can make a world of difference for the people we love.

GETTING CAUGHT

Beliefs: I don't have time now, but I can always get to it later. Not many of us really want to think about our mortality, but it's there, just under the surface. It starts in our teenage years when we think, "Nothing bad is going to happen to me!" I can tell you from personal experience, it can. It does.

Excuses: "Life is just too busy right now." In spite of all the efficiencies – the dishwashers, microwave, the GPS to get us around traffic delays, computer technology, emailing instead of writing letters, etc. – we never seem to have time for everything. We've built in some amazing excuses.

Actions: Procrastinating. Putting things off is not a new phenomenon. However, modern Americans have found new ways of procrastinating that make everything that came before the Information Technology age pale by comparison.

Results: Tragedy can strike at any time. We can keep putting things off, but eventually time catches up. Cemeteries are full of people who had other plans that day.

Getting caught in quicksand is an interesting phenomenon. It's nothing like those old Westerns or *Lone Ranger* episodes where somebody steps into what appears to be dry sand and begins sinking slowly, struggling to get out. You slip down, like you're in a thick pile of mud, and suddenly can't move.

You're walking along, content, your mind on the much-needed date-night out with your spouse you had recently, the pressures at work, or even the frustrations you're feeling at home, and suddenly your feet simply aren't moving anymore. The ground is rising up at you.

Your legs can barely move and every effort drags you deeper and deeper. If no one finds you on a hot day, your life can suddenly be in danger.

That's what it can feel like when you face unexpected circumstances. It doesn't have to be that way, though. Most of the time, people can see quicksand if they know what to look for.

When you're building your life, planning for retirement, don't let excuses get in the way. Don't hang your hat on some belief that because you're strong and healthy today that tomorrow is guaranteed. And don't assume that just because you went through that physical, everything is just fine. My new hero, David Goggins – a retired United States Navy SEAL, American ultramarathon runner, ultra-distance cyclist, triathlete, world record pull-up holder, and best-selling author of *Can't Hurt Me* – nearly died due to a congenital heart defect doctors found during a routine medical checkup. This happened to a man who is considered to be one of the fittest and toughest on the planet. There are countless stories like these when perfectly healthy people suddenly pass away. Thousands upon thousands of men and women across the country will not survive today, even though they appear to be in good health.

> **Don't hang your hat on some belief that because you're strong and healthy today that tomorrow is guaranteed**

The best we can do is accept our mortality, take whatever measures are necessary to give our bodies the best chance to stay alive for as long as possible, and take active steps to protect the people we love the most in the event something does happen to us.

Most of us are not going to have a Nancy to be kind and gracious. Make time and get that stuff done now!

YOUR TURN

Let's take another look at your life. Keep things in perspective. Pull out your guidebook and complete Activity #8.

This is another opportunity to begin diving deep down to the roots and see how your beliefs are impacting your financial life.

CHAPTER 11

Reason Six:
Our Kids Won the Jackpot While We Carried the Slot Machines on Our Backs

It's easy to look at a strong company – manufacturing, advertising, whatever it may be – and see the obvious: success. It's not always easy to see the years of sacrifice, struggle, scrimping and saving, living on peanut butter and jelly sandwiches (and perhaps some ramen noodles for good measure), skipping vacations and cutting others short, negotiations with banks, lenders, suppliers, partners, and the list goes on and on. All this to survive the week or to the end of the month or until that next big invoice *finally* gets paid.

Behind nearly every success story in business is a long and difficult road, one that could have turned out differently had a few things gone wrong or a couple decisions been altered.

Jensen Pipe and Supply was the largest company of its kind in San Diego at its peak. Owners Bubba and Jean were swiftly cruising through their 60s, and retirement was beckoning. But they had a problem.

A major problem.

I'd gotten to know Bubba and Jean quite well through years managing the pension plan for their company and offering other personal financial advice. They were great people. Bubba was tall, wider than some trees, and gentle. He had a refreshing sense of humor – and considering the amount of pressure he felt daily from business affairs, it was that much more amazing.

Jean was a solid force on their team. She was a diligent leader and always ready and willing to roll up her sleeves and get right into the mix of physical labor when necessary. Neither Bubba nor Jean ever viewed themselves as being better than any of their employees.

All-in-all, awesome people.

They loved their three children, and those kids were a primary reason they devoted the best of 25 back-breaking, sweat-inducing years of their lives to building this company. They skipped vacations for 20 of those years, and when they finally managed to scrape together two weeks for their 25th wedding anniversary, the vacation was cut short. They claimed it was a crisis at the company, but I suspect they were just bored and missed their busy life.

Jean often considered Jensen Pipe and Supply to be her fourth child, and she was the type of mother who defended her children ferociously.

Their kids, Deitre, Donny, and Tom, hadn't had a lavish lifestyle growing up, but they hadn't wanted for anything, either. All three headed off to college, but none of them finished. Like nearly a third of U.S. undergraduates, they dropped out.

They were unmotivated, and as the business was finally pulling in solid revenue, they were reaping the benefits from Mom and Dad. Bubba and Jean would essentially hand them whatever they needed, whenever it was required, even for what many might consider hare-brained ideas or ridiculous expenses.

Not all of their ideas were bad. Deitre wanted to set up a spa in Carlsbad, about 20 minutes north of San Diego. A decent idea, especially considering the affluence in the area. However, Deitre lacked business sense, experience, and focus.

Meanwhile Tom's nickname was "Tommy Boy," which may give you some perspective on how others saw him if you know the movie by that name. Tom was into surfing and snowboarding. He had unpolished plans for a clothing line, but beyond a general idea, he never did any work to bring it to life.

When called on to help at Jensen Pipe and Supply, not one of the children would show up on time, and it was even odds they'd show up at all. Each one of them floundered in jobs outside of Jensen. Sometimes they'd quit in a huff; other times they'd be told to leave. There were instances where they'd simply stop showing up. Most of their time was spent sleeping in, going out drinking and partying with friends, and doing as little as possible to help Mom and Dad. They were close in age and had the typical relationship one might expect of teenagers: they argued and got snippy with one another but were still there for each other if any one of them was attacked from the outside.

I saw the kids go from their closing days of high school through to their late 20s and found little to be impressed by. Bubba and Jean dreamed of handing this company to their kids and having it remain solid for generations, for their children and grandchildren and even great-grandchildren.

Realistically, few companies survive the onslaught of time, let alone a changing of the guard, but the way Bubba and Jean built Jensen Pipe and Supply, there was no reason to expect anything short of decades of prosperity. I remember thinking one afternoon that it would take sheer incompetence, blatant disregard, or criminal behavior to bring Jensen down within 20 years.

Bubba kept talking about "grooming" the kids to take over, and even though the kids all waxed poetic about it, claiming they were all-in and wanted nothing more than to keep this company thriving, they wouldn't show up. Every effort Bubba made was met with resistance. They were out of town or unavailable. Their favorite reply seemed to be "Yeah, Dad, I'll stop by next week."

I knew it stung. And I knew Bubba realized this was setting up to be a major problem.

These three adult children had short bursts of energy when it came to business ideas they'd conjured up, but they would last only a couple of weeks, at most, before losing interest. Deitre might have been the one ray of hope among the kids, but it was dim to begin with. Two of these children spent short stints in jail for misdemeanor offenses (DUI for one, minor drug possession for another).

To these three adults, Jensen Pipe and Supply was taking care of them and would do so for life. It was the largest business of its kind in the region and growing. The staff were dedicated and hard-working. And their mom and dad were going to keep on running the show, even though they'd turned 70 and it was clearly time to retire.

As time marched on, Bubba and Jean became more frustrated with their children. Month after month, year after year, they kept prodding the kids to come in and start learning how to take over. Month after month, year after year, those kids kept making excuses.

By the time Bubba turned 75, they decided their time at the company was up. They had not just a business to think about but a team of dedicated employees, some of whom had been with them from the beginning. Bubba was dealing with a growing number of health issues, and Jean's arthritis was making work more difficult.

Bubba had also begun struggling with his memory, which turned out to be early signs of dementia. That's when they decided to sell. Their company was valued at over $20 million. If they gave each of their children an equal share when Bubba and Jean passed away, each would have held more money than most people earn in a lifetime.

But when the kids heard this idea to sell, they went into hysterics.

"How can you sell this?" they asked.

"Why wouldn't you consult us about this first?"

"This was supposed to be ours when you retired!"

These comments were an insult. I'm not sure how Bubba and Jean took them, but when they recounted this episode, their pain was evident.

Some of those remarks were followed by, *"You promised"* and *"This is our dream"* and *"We want to keep this business in the family!"*

What was hidden behind their false concern was a simple truth: their expected inheritance wouldn't come for 10 or 20 years. In the meantime, with the business sold and no longer in the family, there would be no more cash on demand. The parental ATM would dry up until Bubba and Jean passed away.

To show they were serious about taking over, the kids actually started showing up. Every day. On time. It seemed like a miracle, but it was nothing but a con.

And it worked.

They managed to convince Bubba and Jean that they were dedicated to the family business. Finally. But Deitre, Donny, and Tom were working diligently not to keep the company going but to outdo each other. They each wanted to be the leader, the president of the company, and they jumped in to show Mom and Dad who was most worthy.

A few months later, Bubba and Jean relented and decided to hand the business over to their children. Financially, Bubba and Jean were set. They didn't need anything more from the business they'd built, and they could retire in comfort. They also had long-term care policies they'd been paying into for years and took advantage of that to move to an assisted living community where they could golf, relax, swim, and get the support and care Bubba would need in the coming years.

Deitre won the title of president. She was the oldest and appeared to be the most competent, but she inspired little confidence. Most of the employees referred to all three as "Dumb, Dumber, and Dumberer."

The decision left a bitter taste for many long-time employees, but once Bubba and Jean signed the paperwork and said their goodbyes, things changed again. None of the kids showed up much after that, and the employees were happier for it.

Bubba and Jean settled into their new lives with new friends, new activities, and a new purpose. They were in a great community and loved it. Then World War III broke out.

Not content with their titles (even though they each received the same monetary compensation), Tommy Boy and Donny began fighting Deitre for control. They started complaining about one another sleeping on the job and stealing cash. Even a sexual harassment claim was filed. It was a mess.

One night, Deitre had the locks changed. This not only frustrated the employees but also caused more tension among the siblings. She reported to her mom and dad that everything was fine, and when the other two shared their own sentiments, the two senior Jensens simply shrugged it off.

"It's no longer our concern," Bubba told them.

Seeing your life's work being torn apart – by your own family – has to be painful. But I think Bubba knew what was going to happen when he handed the company over to them. Jean knew it as well. At 75, when they made this decision, they had been out of time, out of energy, and out of fight.

One of the children soon began fudging the numbers and the financials. And soon thereafter they fired their long-term accountant, which raised more than a few eyebrows. Some of the other long-time employees called to let Bubba know what was happening, but he could only thank them for their concern and apologize for what was happening. It was out of his hands.

Deitre disappeared on more than a few occasions. Once she called from Italy to check in on things. The business was falling apart.

Their competitors knew it, too. One employee Tommy fired because he was standing up to their incompetence shifted to a main competitor and revealed the chaos that was ensuing at Jensen. The competitor pounced on the opportunity.

What Bubba and Jean had built over the course of 30 years couldn't survive 3 brief years under their children's control. It was an ugly display of incompetence, rivalry, animosity, laziness, and fraud.

I received calls from employees more frequently as the months pressed on. They were concerned about their pension plans. After a few more of these calls, I decided it was time to meet with Bubba and Jean in person.

They cared about their former employees, they cared about what was happening to their company, but there was nothing they could do. "We did everything we could," Bubba said finally. "It's in their hands now and we are focused on ourselves."

He asked me to do what I could to protect and oversee the continuation of the retirement plan. "If something doesn't change soon," I told him, "that could be out of my hands."

Fortunately, as the pressure mounted, and even though these children hated one another by this point, they all agreed to sell. What had been valued at $20 million when they took over had to be let go of for under $3 million. It was a fire sale. Even the property went for far less than they should have been able to get.

Their debts were too high, and their incompetence and deception too overwhelming. The office manager ended up taking over the day-to-day operations, but he wasn't equipped for the responsibility and later quit out of frustration. At such a low sale price, the kids didn't really get much from the sale once debts, taxes, suppliers, and attorney fees were calculated, which came as quite a shock to them. They didn't merely go back to their old lifestyles – they'd never had to work for anything before – so they suddenly had to take a crash course on how to earn a living. Having to start over and support yourself for the first time when you're in your 30s puts you *way* behind the curve.

Bubba and Jean had transitioned to a nursing home by this time. They eventually passed away, leaving what remained of their assets to their children. That equaled $2 million, split three ways. Most times, an inheritance will last about three years. Rumor had it, these adults burned through theirs in less than two.

The money was gone. Deitre, Tom, and Donny had no real skills with which to support themselves. They threatened one another with frivolous lawsuits, but nothing ever came of them. They loathed each other and blamed one another for the failures their lives had become.

I didn't hear from the Jensen children again except for a rumor that Tommy Boy was sleeping on a couch at a friend's apartment. All three had expected to be taken care of for life by the financial windfall handed to them by their parents. All three found themselves struggling, and who knows where they ended up?

I hope they found the ability, desire, and motivation to pick their lives up from the ashes. It doesn't happen often, though.

Attitudes and apathy are hard to change, especially when they've been ingrained for so long, and especially when there's always someone there to provide for them. Deitre, Tommy, and Donny were set up for life, but they weren't established for it. That was the problem. They acquired no skills and lacked motivation because they didn't need them. They were programmed to fail by their parents due to their overabundance of entitlement. The foundation of their life was planted on sand and it all washed away.

Jensen Pipe and Supply is a ghost of a memory now. I wonder how many other companies are in this position, being left to adult children who only want to float through life ... one step away from bankruptcy.

THE BREAKDOWN

Trap Six:
Up in Smoke

 BELIEFS: I want to set my kids up for life. I'll use money as a tool for parenting, because money can buy love and happiness.

 EXCUSES: "I feel guilty because I didn't give them enough attention."

 ACTIONS: Giving your kids everything they want.

 RESULTS: Everything you built including your family is destroyed and the only remains are painful memories. Your good intentions destroyed the will of your kids, robbed them of prosperity and killed their ambition.

There are many things we can devote our time to, but the ones we devote the majority of our time to ultimately become our treasures. We're so inundated with powerful and well-crafted marketing messages that we come to believe happiness comes in the form of material possessions.

Some people purchase the best of everything, creating a home that resembles more of a museum than a place where people live.

Their focus is on the wrong things, the things that don't provide true, lasting happiness. Sure, it's great to enjoy nice things, but sometimes those things become more important than relationships.

Bubba and Jean devoted their attention in life to their business. They sacrificed vacations, their kids' school and sporting events, and even dinners together.

A result of that focus on the business was guilt about not being the kind of parents they wished they'd been. Unfortunately, they didn't realize that until later in life. The irony was that they had been devoted to the business for their children's benefit. Their *Belief* was that they should leave their children better off than they were and money was their way of showing love.

Because of that guilt, they made *Excuses.* They took on this idea that they owed it to their children to give them whatever they wanted and leave them a solid successful business, even in the face of evidence the kids were incapable, unqualified, or even hostile to the idea of taking over.

Their *Action* was to hand over the business despite the warning signs. Bubba and Jean ignored the problems that were evident, especially as they approached the time they wanted to retire. They kept putting off retirement, and even though they had loyal staff – some of whom had been working for them since the beginning – they didn't take the staff's needs into account. They were focused on making up for whatever mistakes they'd made with their children.

None of this happened in a bubble or overnight. Deitre, Donny, and Tom had given more than enough indicators that they were a bad business investment. Time and again they failed, burned through money, and had no respect for any of it – money *or* the business.

When children grow up getting everything they want, what does that do to them? It all depends on the individual, but some people develop a sense of entitlement.

They believe they're owed something.

They think it's easy to get things, to have the best comforts and luxuries. They think that Mom and Dad will simply bail them out if they screw up (again).

It's another form of enabling that these types of parents do, and it's destructive. However, parents struggle with the idea that if they don't support an adult child, it doesn't reflect well on them as people. I know Bubba and Jean wrestled with these issues for a long time, but because they couldn't go back and start over, they felt they had no choice.

I can't be certain, but I always got the sense Bubba and Jean expected things to be easier a lot sooner. I feel they thought the business would take off while their children were still young, when the family could have spent more quality time together.

That didn't happen. When building a business, it rarely ever does.

Some people are workaholics by nature; they're driven by this need to be busy, focusing on financial success and independence, and they keep the blinders on for years and years, one day finally looking up and realizing they missed too many moments in their children's lives. This focus, which was meant to be for the children's benefit, actually hurt Jean and Bubba in the end. The ***Result*** was that the company fell apart and so did the children.

GETTING CAUGHT

 Beliefs: I want to set my kids up for life. I'll use money as a tool for parenting, because money can buy love and happiness. Where does it say that parents need to (or should) take care of their kids for life? What parenting book declares that children deserve better than what their parents had? Just as the Declaration of Independence declares, we all have the right to the pursuit of happiness but not the guarantee of it.

 Excuses: "I feel guilty because I didn't give them enough attention." Giving into the demands of children can stem from guilt or love or a combination. Do it once, get accolades and a sense of love, and it's easier for it to become habitual.

139

Actions: Giving your kids everything they want. Bubba and Jean refused to see the signs of incompetence and immaturity within their children. They noticed it. They ignored it. They justified it. If they had confronted it, there's no way they could have handed the reins of their business to Deitre, Donny, or Tom with a clear conscience.

Results: Everything you built including your family is destroyed and the only remains are painful memories. Your good intentions destroyed the will of your kids, robbed them of prosperity and killed their ambition. Forty years of hard work – striving, saving, sacrificing – all went up in smoke. They knew it was going to happen. I'm sure they also knew the kind of lives their children would have in the wake of that disaster. By that time, though, there was really nothing else they could do.

One of the most important jobs a parent has is to build character within their children. Handing them everything they want, giving in to temper tantrums just to bring about peace for a few moments, buying them a brand-new car because they "won't be caught dead in a used piece of junk" are just a few examples of the spoiling mentality to which Americans have grown far too accustomed.

But making your kids' lives easy can handicap them. It's not what you do for them but what you've taught them to do for themselves that will make them successful human beings. Struggle, sacrifice, and even pain

> **Struggle, sacrifice, and even pain can all help build character. Hard work, earning one's keep, and learning discipline are the true pillars of success. These are the tools and gifts children of all ages need from an early age.**

can all help build character. Hard work, earning one's keep, and learning discipline are the true pillars of success. These are the tools and gifts children of all ages need from an early age.

There are going to be times when people slip and fall, when they completely fail, and that's when family and friends should step up and help. But bailing someone out should not become a lifetime pattern. A safety net shouldn't become a hammock, and raising a strong, mature, independent child doesn't mean creating a cradle-to-grave entitlement system.

What is living with their parents into their 30s and even 40s doing for adult children? Do they gain a sense of responsibility? What about personal accountability? There may be times when adult children need a hand, have bottomed out, but supporting them this way becomes a crutch.

We're warned not to feed wild animals because they'll become dependent on it and no longer scavenge or hunt for their own food. In other words, they'll become weaker as a result. The same concept applies here.

It can be exciting to hit the jackpot at the casino or win the lottery. But without personal accountability and responsibility, with a poor set of beliefs, in most cases everything falls apart in a matter of time and you step firmly into the B.E.A.R. Trap. In truth, most people who inherit businesses or win a jackpot without a good attitude and quality character in place first generally lose it within a few years.

It's fine and normal to want your children to have a better life than you, but you need to understand the limits on charity and support. Building character doesn't happen overnight.

Keep in mind, too … the strongest sailors are not made on calm seas. They need to get through the storm themselves and when they do, they'll be better for it.

YOUR TURN

Let's take another look at your life. Keep things in perspective. Pull out your guidebook and complete Activity #9.

This is another opportunity to begin diving deep down to the roots and see how your beliefs are impacting your financial life.

CHAPTER 12

Reason Seven:
The Double J

Twenty-five some odd years had slipped away before I crossed paths with an old, dear friend from childhood. It was a bright, early Saturday morning as I strolled down a long beach path, surfboard tucked comfortably under my arm. I spotted an old Volkswagen van. It was an early 1970s model that one would expect to have flowers and peace symbols decorating its façade.

This van showed its age. A bit of rust, more than a few dents and dings, and a well-worn and faded exterior highlighted a difficult existence. I studied the vehicle because it was similar to the type I had driven during my high school and early college days. A sense of nostalgia floated around as I remembered tossing my surfboard in the back during those days, sand, food, empty cans, beach towels, and other miscellaneous items strewn about.

Friends had long since come and gone, but the memories lingered. In a flash, I was recalling people I hadn't thought about or seen in decades.

I spotted a gentleman about my age, but holding the well-worn appearance of somebody perhaps five or 10 years older, emerge from the van. A boy about 12 or 13 slid out from somewhere behind it. I stopped short, my eyes narrowed, and realization dawned upon me. I recognized this man.

Quickly my brain began calculating the number of years that must have transpired between the last time we had a conversation or even stood face to face with one another. It was Kimo, one of my better friends from those early childhood years. We spent many days and some nights along the beach surfing, laughing, and joking around.

Could it be? I pondered. *What a strange coincidence.*

If this truly was Kimo, seeing him here, after all this time, on this stretch of beach almost seemed too great a coincidence. When the man turned and spotted me picking up my stride, he did a double take. Our eyes locked and we immediately understood the connection.

Smiles stretched across our faces and my surfboard began to slip from my grip as I slowed and came to a stop just a few feet away from him. I let the board rest on the ragged salt-air saturated grass. The young boy hovered nearby, but not next to my old friend.

"Kimo," I said with some excitement. "I can't believe it's you?"

"Johnny Mac," he replied. "What's up? How long's it been? It's so good to see you."

We estimated somewhere around 20 years, but that wasn't entirely true. It had been at least 30 since we hung out as good, close friends, but as high school took hold and we began circling different groups of friends, pursuing various interests that tore us apart, our interactions flickered out until the last time I remembered seeing him was at a high school party and I questioned whether he even recognized me or would remember it.

He introduced the boy as his nephew, but it was evident there was some strain in that relationship. I had no idea what was going on, but as Kimo was in his full surfing gear and his little sidekick was toting a smaller version of a surfboard behind him, I presumed we were all there for the same reason.

We fell into a collective stride that turned and descended a few steps down toward a rocky beach below. We talked and reminisced quickly while heading into the water. Back in the day we played football in the streets, went body surfing, boogie boarding, surfing, saw plenty of movies in Waikiki, and we even shared a paper route. When we were young, there was almost nothing we didn't do together. They were wonderful memories and as the warm Pacific waters nestled in around my toes and strolled up my ankle and toward my knee, my smile was genuine.

It was truly wonderful to see Kimo after all this time.

I noticed he hadn't changed much through these years, aside from the deep lines along his face and the signs of well-worn, textured skin and thinning hair. But there was something different about his demeanor, his appearance, and his stature. It appeared as though he had a limp but aside from an occasional grimace, he hid whatever bothered him well.

Growing up, Kimo was what we would consider a rich kid. Though he never carried himself with any disdain or elevated status, his father was well-off. He lived in a luxurious house on the beach. He and his older brother always had the best clothes. But that day, on the beach, noticing the fraying edges of his suit and the surfboards he and his nephew carried that had seen better days, something wasn't adding up.

The outline or sketch of this old friend of mine was the same, but there was something different about him. I couldn't put it into words at that time, but as we paddled out toward the breaks, rested on our surfboards waiting for the right set, we chatted, reminisced, and a flood of memories poured in; a torrential downpour on a scalding summer's day.

His father was a major developer on the islands. When we were kids, he was building luxury homes, high-end properties for the wealthiest of the wealthy. He had his proverbial business hand in numerous endeavors across all the islands of Hawaii. He also had vested interests in some dealings on the mainland.

Kimo was the prototypical popular teenager. He was an incredibly talented artist and just about everyone recognized it, even in his earliest years. The drawings he would quickly sketch in class and those he took more time to focus on at home were inspiring. There was a time long after high school when I remember speaking to a fellow classmate and our conversation mentioned Kimo briefly. He had taken his talents and become successful in California. That's what we heard.

I was happy for him. Proud, actually.

Kimo never had to worry about money. He always had enough cash for whatever it was he wanted to do and he was often more than willing to pay for me and some other friends if we didn't.

One of the last times I actually saw Kimo in person before that day on the beach was at the aforementioned party. He didn't seem to really recognize me, though. He had a beer in one hand and a joint in the other. His mind was completely oblivious to almost everything going on around me.

We shared a quick but awkward hello and he hurried off. I wondered if he had felt embarrassed for me seeing him like that, but as teenagers, I dismissed that quickly.

Kimo was a great athlete. He was an exceptional swimmer and a water polo player. For anyone who knows anything about water polo, you have to be in peak physical condition and have incredible stamina to compete in that sport. He was offered a scholarship to a small school on the West Coast, but he turned it down.

With great looks, a charming smile, and plenty of charisma, he was popular with the girls. He could disarm the best of us with a well-timed joke. In short, if you get the idea I envied him or I was proud to be his friend, you would be correct on both counts. But that envy had nothing to do with jealousy – just being glad to be his friend.

Kimo's older brother was a wonderful influence. I always assumed Kimo would experiment with a variety of career options or even business opportunities with his brother's encouragement and guidance. Unfortunately, because of his father's dedication to his career and their mother seeming to focus on things other than raising children, they grew up with far too much latitude.

They also had far too much access to their parents' liquor cabinet.

I spent about an hour catching a few decent waves, wiping out more than I care to admit, and since surfing never turned into an obsession like it was for so many others in Hawaii, after an hour or so at a stretch I usually cried uncle and called it a day. I told Kimo it was great seeing him and that it was a pleasure meeting his nephew. I said I would love to get together and hang out and catch up, and his reply was, "Shoots! Let's do it."

I got his contact information and a few days later reached out. I was surprised; he actually did want to sit down and talk. Too often these platitudes from old, long-forgotten friends are nothing more than niceties. This was different. We decided to grab coffee at the Kahala Mall.

I got there first and when Kimo finally showed up, I was ready to order a refill on my coffee. He was dressed exactly the way I had seen him the other morning. I stood and we embraced and then sat down to catch up.

I sensed a nervous energy surrounding Kimo. He seemed extremely anxious to talk, to share what he'd been up to all those years. It was almost as if he needed somebody to hear his story. In my career, I've discovered that many people desperately want someone to listen to their tale, usually a tale of woe, trouble, suffering, and mistakes, and that person more often than not seems to be me.

What I was about to hear was not even close to the typical story I'm exposed to through my career, though. What Kimo recounted to me came across as more like a Hollywood exposé or riches to rags tale that would make great fodder for a powerful TV special or full-length feature film.

It didn't take long for Kimo to recount the episodes and situations of his life.

Following high school, Kimo headed off to Santa Monica to a community college. He dropped out after the first semester. He was an artist at heart and between classes and trying to figure out the best way to study for exams, he accepted who he was and what he wanted to do.

He didn't have to worry about money. At this point in his life, his father was more than willing to fund just about any project, endeavor, or adventure Kimo pursued. He was proud of his son and his talents and he wanted to help him out, perhaps to a fault. I'm sure it made his father feel good on some level to contribute, and as I've seen in many other situations, it might have assuaged some of the guilt for not having been there enough during the formative years.

His father funded this new art endeavor, and it was no waste. Remember I mentioned hearing about him finding success in Los Angeles after we graduated high school? Yep, Kimo was quickly recruited to paint, draw, and do graphic design and a number of other artistic projects for a wide range of people and businesses. It didn't take long for his talents to precede his name and he started building an incredible reputation throughout Southern California.

Vastly wealthy people, even celebrities, were paying good money for him to do what he thoroughly loved.

At the time, he admitted to me in that café, he was a periodic drinker and more periodic pot smoker. All of this started during the earliest days of our high school career, about the time we had both begun drifting apart. It wasn't his drinking or smoking that drove us part, mind you, nor was our diverging paths any reason for his decision to start. Mine was football and track. His was water polo, surfing, and art. I don't believe true friendships ever truly end; sometimes they just go on hiatus.

Over time, finding all this success, the drinking and smoking slowly crept in on him, squeezing him more and more each day. He soon found himself consuming alcohol and smoking a joint at least a few times every day.

As with most addictions, what worked yesterday might not have the same effect tomorrow and that usually leads to the need for stronger substances. While he was living in L.A. and finding all that success early on, he began consuming what he called "The Double J" – basically "Jack Daniels and a Joint." He believed this brought out his creativity.

His isn't the only story that mirrors this type of idea. Numerous rock stars, actors, writers and even highly successful professionals have reported feeling a sense of enlightenment or improvement in their craft when they were feeling the buzz or 'high' of alcohol and drugs. For most of them, however, that sense of performing at a higher level is only an illusion.

Kimo told me that his Jack and a Joint habit not only became habitual, it started earlier and earlier each day. It reached a point when he couldn't get out of bed or get started without it.

Around the same time, he was being invited to celebrity parties and his artwork was gaining more and more attention and exposure. It was at one of these parties when he was exposed to cocaine for the first time. He said it was a famous actress who lured him in. Kimo looked embarrassed, but truthful when he said he felt he had no power to say no, nor did he have any real desire. He was caught up in the accolades and the company that surrounded him. He leaned in and said to me, "John, I couldn't say no to her."

He admitted that he felt this was not just the greatest, but simultaneously the worst thing that ever happened to him. I found it incredibly odd to hear somebody say cocaine and drugs was a great thing, but at the time he felt this was elevating his craft, his art, and his career.

He was in the middle of celebrity circles, partying with the elite of the elite, and he didn't see how that party could ever end.

Five years after venturing to L.A. and building this amazingly profitable career, Kimo's father passed away. His parents had long been divorced by then and therefore he and his brother were on the receiving end of an inheritance that, in one word, was massive. He admitted it was just over $10 million. I wasn't all that surprised, but those kinds of numbers still stun me when people talk about them as though they're everyday things.

Although he was making good money with his artwork, this new influx of money gave him permission, in his mind, to slack off on his work. He spent more time partying and less time working. He was getting well entrenched in the Hollywood lifestyle. After all, when you have a mountain of money land on top of you, when you think it's never going to end, what need could there be to work?

The drugs took over every aspect of his life. He reached a point when he could no longer function or produce anything worthwhile. Even the work he had been commissioned to do was being rejected. Instead of examining himself with these rejections, he dismissed them and dove deeper into his addictions. Cocaine had become his new passion and priority.

With his new inheritance, Kimo purchased an impressive mansion in Hollywood, neighboring some of the biggest stars in the industry. He wasn't the type of person who needed 10,000 square feet (for the space or the ego), a pool that resembled one at a waterpark, or other amenities; he admitted he only did that to feel as though he was still relevant.

He wasn't.

Every morning, Kimo admitted, he would wake up and say this was it, he was taking charge, that his addiction was over, but by 10am he was back in the throes of the Double J, the cocaine, and anything else he needed to stay high. It reached a point when one day he felt as though he was having a heart attack. A neighbor spotted him staggering outside, his face colorless and ghastly and looking like the walking dead. He was rushed to the hospital and then immediately sent to detox. He ended up at a high end, incredibly expensive rehabilitation center for 45 days. It was supposed to be 90 days, but he felt he had been rehabilitated and left early. He was wrong.

By the time he returned home, not only were the bills mounting, he had exhausted more than two-thirds of his inheritance. He tried to dive back into his artwork, but the pressure was too much. His creativity had suffered and with each rejection not only was he losing his reputation, he was turning back to the substances that helped artificially lift him up previously. He had been so reliant on drugs and alcohol to get him through the day that he became ill-equipped to produce and perform the way he used to prior to his addictions. Essentially, he became useless. It wasn't long before he completely crashed emotionally and then tragedy ensued. He was involved in a horrible car accident.

The personal and financial damage was immense. Because he was under the influence, he spent 30 days in jail and a fortune on legal fees, ultimately agreeing to a large settlement with the driver he hit. Kimo broke his back in the accident and because of his wealth he never assumed he would need health insurance. He always joked and referred to himself as Mr. Invincible. Lying in the hospital bed and pain recovery while in jail proved otherwise.

He underwent numerous surgeries, hundreds of physical therapy sessions, chiropractors, acupuncture, and so much more, but the pain never receded.

That was when another demon entered his life: OxyContin.

I've heard this story so many times that it still boggles my mind how many people get hooked on and wrapped up in pain medications like Oxy or Percocet. The victims of this drug say it's impossible to understand the allure without having been exposed to it yourself.

Kimo told me in the café that afternoon that his addiction was so out of control he reached the point of downing upwards of 40 pills a day. It was hard to fathom.

Everyone and anyone who tried to convince him he had a problem he drove away and instead turned to the company of a like-minded associate. This friend had a similar story to Kimo's; his father was a movie business mogul, incredibly wealthy, and essentially nonexistent. It wasn't until this friend died of an overdose that Kimo was shaken to the core and finally decided enough was enough.

The inheritance was gone. Every penny. He was in massive debt and decided to walk away from everything, including that mansion. One morning he walked out the door with just the clothes on his back and left the key on the front stoop. The bank would take care of the rest.

He couldn't paint because his hands were shaking all the time. The pain in his back wouldn't allow him to stand or sit still for long stretches at a time. He rented a small studio on a weekly basis, grabbed a few odd jobs wherever he could just to pay those bills, and fought his addiction. Not long after this all transpired, he called his sister-in-law back in Hawaii. Even though she and his brother had long since divorced, he had always had a great relationship with her and considered her his true sister.

She offered him a place to stay on her couch while he got back on his feet, but she had two conditions: First, no substances. Ever.

He hopped on the next plane.

The second was that he had to not only attend, but become involved in the church. Coincidentally, he had already been thinking about this. He admitted he began watching various television ministries and the message began to sink in.

His life began to change. He was in a new environment, facing strict rules, and had a new purpose. He took on yoga and meditation and discovered that both helped his mental and physical body in ways he couldn't have foreseen. His nephew played a key role in his recovery, too, as Kimo was determined to be a role model for this young man.

In that café on that warm summer day, Kimo stopped, paused, and looked down at the space between us. After a few silent moments, his gaze lifted up to me.

"John," he said. "It was God and yoga that saved my life."

As he confessed this story to me I didn't interrupt once. I couldn't. I was enthralled. It was sad and painful and upsetting yet fascinating to hear this tragic and hopeful story of somebody I admired and always considered a friend. It was tragic to realize just how much pain he had gone through. Yes, he caused it himself, but his story was truly the stuff of best-selling books and movies.

I mentioned he should write a memoir and he laughed. "Yeah, maybe one day. For now I'm focused on changing my life."

When he finished, bringing us full circle to the time when he strolled through that café to unload all this on me, I asked him plainly, "What happened? How did this all start? What was the tipping point?"

He thought about it, but only a brief moment, and then said, "It was that first beer, that first joint, that first snort of cocaine. Those 'firsts' destroyed my life."

He said it was a long, slippery slope but he never felt himself sliding. He always thought he was rising or climbing when he was, in fact, falling. One thing led to another, then another, then another.

He said the best analogy is that of the fly and the carnivorous pitcher plant. The smell of nectar draws flies to it like honey does to bees. This nectar tastes so good that the flies cannot resist its allure.

Unfortunately, the meal isn't free.

As the fly continues downward, it becomes oblivious to the peril it will soon face. It gets to the point it has gorged itself so much it can't move. Its legs and arms are coated with sticky nectar and the more it struggles the more it gets stuck. And very soon, the pitcher plant will drown the fly and consume it.

When he reached a point that the beer no longer fulfilled him, he added marijuana. When that no longer satisfied, it was hard liquor. Then it was cocaine, then combinations of these drugs, and then, ultimately, pain pills. He quoted Huey Lewis when he said, "It was at that point I needed a new drug."

Drugs and alcohol destroyed his life, his relationships, his health, his family, and it was why he lost more than $10 million. Well, as Kimo would admit, it wasn't the drugs and alcohol that destroyed his life, but his choices that led to the addiction and his

> **Addiction is an insidious spiral that quietly and casually strolls into your life, whispers in your ear that everything will be better with just one more, and then suddenly it launches you into hell**

choices that allowed him to stay there.

He confided in me that addiction is an insidious spiral that quietly and casually strolls into your life, whispers in your ear that everything will be better with just one more, and then suddenly it launches you into hell.

"You would be absolutely surprised by the number of doctors, lawyers, judges, executives – people from all walks of life who are dealing with these things, John. I saw them in my counseling sessions. It affects everyone."

I tried to offer him some consolation, some reassurance. "You still have your life. You live in Hawaii, you're back with family, you found God. You actually seem happy." Then I added, with a smile, "And you have one awesome looking surf-mobile."

He leaned in and quietly said, just for my ears, "That's where I live."

He was teaching yoga and though that didn't pay very well, it was getting a bit too crowded at his sister-in-law's house. He was content for now. He said the important thing was that he's living each and every day under God's watchful eye, sober, and seeking some way to help others.

He lost every dollar, but for Kimo it could have been worse. He could've lost every breath.

Trap Seven: Addiction

 BELIEFS: I'm in control. I'm invincible.

 EXCUSES: "I don't have to worry because nothing's going to hurt me."

 ACTIONS: Failing to acknowledge the long-term risks of alluring substances.

 RESULTS: Getting caught in the lure of drugs and alcohol and losing everything.

On June 1, 2009, Air France Flight 447 took off from Rio de Janeiro, heading for Paris. The aircraft crashed into the Atlantic Ocean with 228 people on board. Investigators would ultimately conclude that inexperienced co-pilots had failed to fully understand various warnings that were triggered by the icing over of pitot tubes. This is a device that's used to measure airspeed and altitude.

When the pitot tubes iced over, the autopilot could no longer accurately measure air speed, and with the pilot out of the cockpit for a restroom break, the copilot angled the nose upward and continued to provide throttle in an effort to regain altitude.

By the time the pilot returned and recognized that they were actually in a stall, it was too late. They thought they were climbing and no longer trusted the instruments.

What Kimo described to me that day in the café is just like this. We can feel as though we're in control, right up until the moment we realize the crash is inevitable. To get out alive is about the only miracle we can hope for at that time.

I believe every one of us has a crutch, some behavior that grabs hold of us (usually early on in life) and refuses to let go. Most of the time we ignore it, possibly even relishing it to feel some comfort, a relief from stress and anxiety. It could be spending time on your smartphone, playing video games, having a few beers or some wine after work, eating sugary snacks, smoking, playing golf, exercising for several hours a day, or just about anything else.

Some people call these *vices,* while others refer to them as habits. We rarely recognize when they start slipping from habits to addictions and ultimately to serious problems.

We don't see these warning signs because we don't recognize them as problems to begin with. After all, every teenager drinks, right? What's the big deal? It's just a video game. What's the harm in playing for a few hours? Meanwhile, those "few hours" can easily turn into 8, 10, or 12 hours straight.

A vice, a habit, a pattern of behavior ... all these things can become problematic over time. If we are not mastering our lives, if we are not focusing on the potential for problems to develop from these simple pleasures, it becomes that much easier to slip into the trap.

> **If we are not mastering our lives, if we are not focusing on the potential for problems to develop from these simple pleasures, it becomes that much easier to slip into the trap.**

Kimo discovered this in just about the toughest way a person can

155

learn these lessons. On their own, his habits of drinking and smoking may not have been big problems, but they masked other issues, emotional challenges, mental fatigue, anxiety, stress, and doubt.

From where he came in life, raised in a family of wealth, having incredible talent in artistic endeavors, there was no reason for him to see anything but invincibility when he looked in the mirror.

My point here is that when a person *feels invincible,* they think they're the master of whatever habits they have.

However, all too often, bad habits and *Belief* systems begin taking over. We believe we're in control and even invincible from any damage these substances may have over us. When that starts, we develop *Excuses* to continue doing the things we want, even if or when we start recognizing a problem developing.

When I was in college, I had a friend in the dorm who started out just like the rest of us, partying on the weekends, but then things started to change. He was drinking more during the week. It may have been one or two or three beers on a Tuesday or Thursday evening, but it progressed.

Before we realized there was a problem, the cans were collecting in almost every space available in his dorm room and overfilling the recycling canister outside.

At 18 years old, he had become an alcoholic. There were other problems going on in his life, with his parents, siblings, girlfriend, failing grades, and more, but he had put on a false front. We'd all believed everything was fine, that he was happy, well-adjusted, and in control.

When we finally confronted him about it, he had the excuses all lined up. "I'm fine. I can quit whenever I want." "I'm just having some fun." "Nothing bad is going to happen to me."

We held an intervention, and we reached out to his family. People made an effort. But by the time we'd recognized the problem, he had already convinced himself he was invincible.

His *Actions* – failing to acknowledge the risks – represented that mentality, and the *Results* were no different from how they've been for thousands of people across the country. Drugs and alcohol destroy lives. They destroy families. They destroy finances.

The last I heard of him, he was broke and still an alcoholic.

GETTING CAUGHT

 Beliefs: I'm in control. I'm invincible. I'm not sure when or where it starts, but many children and teenagers honestly think nothing bad will happen to them. They see their whole lives ahead of them and never consider it could be over within minutes. Death doesn't have to be physical, though, when your life crashes down around you. Sometimes the problem starts with an invincible attitude, but often it starts with insecurity, doubt, fear, or anxiety.

 Excuses: "I don't have to worry because nothing's going to hurt me." Because of that belief in invincibility, the excuses become polished. Since nothing's going to hurt you, what's the harm in doing anything?

 Actions: Failing to acknowledge the long-term risks of alluring substances. People start leaping before they look. Perhaps insecurity drives the decision to try the next drug of choice, or an accident leads to an over-prescription of pain medications. When we don't properly assess the risks, the threat of falling rises.

 Results: Getting caught in the lure of drugs and alcohol and losing everything. Drugs and alcohol destroy lives. They destroy families. They destroy finances.

Not everyone gets the opportunity to return home. In this case, *home* could be a second chance at life. *Home* could be a spouse who ultimately takes you back. *Home* could be your career. *Home* could be your life.

Read the tabloids or turn on celebrity news programs – they almost always tell the same story with different names: men and women who had fame and fortune but fell into a world of depravity, drugs, alcohol, and addictions of all sorts and continued to spend and spend and spend until there was nothing left.

Addiction is an epidemic, and it doesn't simply affect the poor, the dropouts, the lonely, or the failures. It affects people from every walk of life, and it continues to destroy the wealth of people who never thought they could ever go broke because of it.

> **Addiction is an epidemic, and it doesn't simply affect the poor, the dropouts, the lonely, or the failures. It affects people from every walk of life.**

The richer a person is when they become addicted to drugs or alcohol, the harder the fall can be. That's because rich people have the resources to mask the symptoms, hiding their problems from even their closest family and friends.

They start tapping into retirement portfolios and hidden savings accounts and racking up massive debts to cover their addiction. Kimo's problems didn't start after the accident and his addiction to pain pills. They didn't start with the company he was keeping in Los Angeles. They didn't start with his growing success in art.

They didn't even start in grade school with that first beer, cigarette, or joint. They started at the root of his belief system: that he was stronger than any problem he could face, even if he felt peer pressure to try something; he was still invincible.

Kimo was lucky. Not everyone is. He lost all his money, his talents, and his friends, but he could have lost his life.

At least he still has another chance.

 YOUR TURN
Let's take another look at your life. Keep things in perspective. Pull out your guidebook and complete Activity #10.

This is another opportunity to begin diving deep down to the roots and see how your beliefs are impacting your financial life.

CHAPTER 13

Reason Eight:
The Big Leagues

You've made it!
You hit the jackpot!
You're an instant millionaire!

Be honest here, do any of those three simple statements get your juices flowing? Do they have the same kind of impact that a well-designed and artfully photographed picture of a chocolate molten lava cake does when you're extremely hungry?

For many of us, they do. In fact, our modern culture has become so addicted to instant riches, overnight millionaire status, and "making the big time" that more and more people are dropping billions of dollars every year on the lottery and flocking to an increasing number of casinos in a growing number of states. The statistics are staggering. Last year American's spent over $72 billion on traditional lottery tickets which equates to $223 per person. It's insane!

Why is this happening? There's this simple idea that, *"If I just had more money, I would be thoroughly and truly happy."*

We have become a culture that honestly believes money is the root of deep-seated happiness. Unfortunately, reality is a much different beast. There are hundreds, thousands, and even tens of thousands of stories of instant millionaires, overnight success stories that crashed and burned.

Some of them led to a permanent end while others lost family, friends, jobs, careers, homes, and their life. Just look at so many lottery winners who now wish they never had won in the first place due to the personal devastation all that newfound money caused.

In this chapter, I wish to share a story about a young man named Joey. He had a promising athletic career and started with the right idea about his finances. A new signing bonus, lucrative contract, and an inheritance, Joey could have set himself up for a life of financial prosperity. Sadly, like so many flooded with instant money, he got caught up in the rush, the lavish lifestyle, and pressure from almost every side within his new social circles.

There are dozens, even hundreds, of examples of famous men and women – athletes, movie stars, musicians, businessmen – who had everything and lost it all. They had more money than most of us could ever imagine possessing, and they ended up in bankruptcy, or worse. I'll provide a list of some of them in the next chapter, but for now, this story is about Joey. He was an all-around great young man – a farm boy from Ohio who had developed incredible skills on the baseball diamond and the football field. As with many young athletes, he was exceedingly popular, with great charisma, a humble attitude, and charming good looks. He had friends in just about every corner of his life.

Even before he graduated high school, in that glorious senior year, he was drafted by the Dodgers, a Major League team. Most high school draftees in the Majors go to the "farm system," which is the developmental arm of the Major Leagues. The Dodger's farm league was a far cry from the rural community in which he had grown up. His first stop was with their Double-A team, the San Antonio Missions. They clearly had good plans for Joey because the signing bonus they offered indicated they expected him to reach the Majors before too long.

It was not even a full season with the Missions before he was sent on to the organization's Triple-A team, the Albuquerque Dukes. Both San Antonio and Albuquerque were a far cry from the hustle-and-bustle of L.A., but were still light years beyond the culture and slow rural pace Joey knew and was comfortable with.

Joey was ambitious, hard-working, and dedicated to his craft. He could have easily earned scholarships for both baseball and football to many major universities, but the diamond was where he longed to be. I hadn't met him at this point, but from what I learned about him in the months and years that followed, at the time he was spending almost every waking moment working out, lifting weights, practicing his hitting and fielding, and honing his skills with his coaches.

It's what I did during the early years of my financial career that eventually brought Joey to my door. I used to submit various financial articles to a downtown Los Angeles business newspaper. I had initially done this with the intention of drawing clients, even though my experience was still minimal. I had been hired by a major Wall Street firm after receiving my first regulatory license which I earned in an evening training program. I hadn't yet completed my college degree, but they took a chance on me. I don't think it was just because I was attending night school, but also my sheer persistence. I was grateful for the opportunity.

Joey reached out and contacted me. He introduced himself as a member of the Dodgers organization. He admitted he had been recently drafted and was working on their farm team. When he first contacted me, he had just moved up to the Dukes. One step from the Majors. His signing bonus was more than fair, especially at that time. It was obvious the Dodgers had high hopes for this young man.

He mentioned that before he'd even trekked out to Los Angeles, his family and some of his closest friends and teachers warned him to be wary of the sharks out there.

Somehow he had seen one or two of my articles and recognized I was working for a reputable firm. He admitted he'd called me – a young man myself at the time – because I wasn't pushing my services in those articles. He had grown instantly wary of the endless parade of lawyers, financial experts, advisers, and investment specialists barraging him with solicitations.

After a few simple questions over the phone, we agreed to meet for lunch at an inexpensive delicatessen. I was drawn to this young man because of his demeanor and humility. He was confident but understood he had little experience in big-city life or even bigger professional contracts. I kept wondering, *Why in the world is this guy trying to work with me?*

We discussed his experience in Albuquerque and why he connected with me, being that I was in Los Angeles.

"John," he said with a boundless energy, "I'm going to get the call. I'll be in L.A. soon. I figured I might as well plan ahead."

I started investigating his professional career trajectory (even as brief as it was to that time) and couldn't find a reason Joey wouldn't make it to the L.A. team. He was working hard, impressing agents and coaches and sports reporters alike. There was a buzz in L.A. baseball circles about this young man, that he was going to be "called up" soon.

During our initial meeting, especially with his coming from a small town, he impressed me with a level head on his shoulders and a keen sense of responsibility. He wanted to do the right thing. He was blown away by L.A.'s size, bustling life, and traffic – and at this time the O.J. Simpson trial was in full swing.

We discussed his experience in Los Angeles during our initial meeting, especially with his coming from a small town. He was blown away by its size, bustling life, and traffic – and at this time the O.J. Simpson trial was in full swing.

I had passed my exams, earned my certification, but I'll admit I was still wet behind the ears. I knew little about the intricacies of financial planning. It takes about six weeks to study for and pass the main securities exam to call yourself a Financial Advisor, but it takes years of dedicated time to develop the invaluable experience that truly makes a difference for your clients. I appreciated my employer, the support they provided, and the mentoring I received during those first years.

I admitted as much to Joey when we met, but he was adamant about working with me. He said it was because I wasn't focused on the millions he was about to earn in the Big Leagues.

We had a great chat over lunch, and I suggested scheduling another meeting with a senior partner of the firm that I had been working with. As he had no doubt he'd make the Big League roster one day, he wanted to make sure his future was set financially.

Sitting down with the two of us in a subsequent meeting at our office a week or two later, Joey laid out his goals. He had received a significant signing bonus, as mentioned, and combined with an inheritance from his grandfather, he had about a $1.5 million start. He stated outright, "I want to put that money away … forever." This was going to be his retirement money so that no matter how much or how little he made in baseball, he would be set for life.

"I don't ever want to touch this," he said. "If I call you for money, you have permission to hang up on me."

I remember looking at my colleague and seeing his impressed expressions. It wasn't every day (in fact, it was almost unheard of) to hear a young, instant-millionaire athlete, superstar, or lotto winner making these kinds of claims.

We also understood that despite his practical nature, it was inevitable he would spend at least some of it. After all, he would need a place to live, a car to drive, and some other items of interest. We recommended he take $1 million and put it under lock and key, invest it in a diversified portfolio, and, figuratively speaking, forget about it until he turns 65. This was a portfolio primarily containing blue-chip stocks with a small allocation of high-quality bonds. Based on historical data, this portfolio was designed to deliver approximately a 7.5% average rate of return over time. The historical average of the overall stock market has been 10%, but because of our small bond allocation, we were now targeting around 7 to 8%. We wanted to be slightly more conservative in our investments than the overall market and we needed to account for taxes and fees. When you do the math, $1 million compounding at 7.5% for 45 years will be worth just shy of $26 million.

As most people would readily admit, $26 million is more money than most of us will earn in our lifetime, probably more than a few lifetimes. A 65-year-old sitting on $26 million, managing it properly, would never have to worry about money again, no matter how much they traveled or experienced in life.

Joey's jaw dropped. I had to show him the figures on the calculator and explain how compounding interest works. I also went into detail about how spending money now will negatively impact his future, regardless of what he may make from a Major League contract.

If he spent $1,000 today, that could have grown to $22,000 by the time he was 40. In less than 20 years, everyone who needlessly spends

$1,000 now could have had an extra $22,000 (or more) in 20 years. Those are sobering numbers.

Joey admitted he had never heard any of this before. "Not a single one of my teachers ever talked about finances like this," he said. I understood because I wasn't taught this in high school, either.

Joey didn't want to leave until his accounts were set up, a plan was established, and we had formulated and implemented an investment strategy. We were on the same page, not to mention excited – having a young, soon-to-be Big League superstar being diligent and responsible with his new wealth was a rare gift.

> In less than 20 years, everyone who needlessly spends $1,000 now could have had an extra $22,000 (or more) in 20 years.

Unfortunately, everything we talked about – even his incredible enthusiasm – evaporated within weeks of his Major League deal.

He returned to Albuquerque and pounded opposing pitchers. His on base percentage, batting average, and fielding prowess were simply unequaled on his team, and in most of the Triple-A league. After a full season in Triple A, Joey got the call he dreamed about from the Dodgers front office.

He was given a two-year initial contract worth a few million dollars. Spring training was a showcase for the young upstart. He jumped out of the gate with a sprint, smacking balls all over the field and creating a greater buzz about his potential.

Joey worked out early in the morning and late at night. He put more time into his work than any other member of the Dodgers organization, and it showed on the field. He gained considerable playing time once the regular season got into full swing and Joey began looking to settle into his new home city.

He purchased a condo in Manhattan Beach, California. That, in and of itself, may not sound like a big deal, but for a young Major Leaguer, it's a significant investment. The bigger problem developed as he spent more time in Hollywood and Beverly Hills, palling around with other players, who were introducing him to swanky parties, celebrities, and a host of men and women who were drawn to those with money or the promise of big bucks.

Because of this new circle of friends, he believed he had to look the part. That meant he went out and spent lavishly on new clothes, a new sports car to replace his "unsightly" RAV4, and, of course, some high-end jewelry, including a Rolex.

Fortunately for Joey, drugs played no part in his life. He was strong enough to avoid the allure, no matter how many people put pressure on him to "just try some." He admitted to me one afternoon that those offers came daily.

In short, Joey had gotten just the slightest taste of the L.A. lifestyle and fell completely in love with it. His new Major League teammates were wrapped up in it, and he felt the need to keep up with their expensive lifestyles.

He went to the best clubs, dropped hundreds of dollars every night, ate at the hippest and most expensive restaurants, and spent lavishly on the women who surrounded him. He later admitted that he ordered food that made him cringe at the sight and smell. He said it made him feel as though he was part of the "in" crowd.

When all this started, his requests to withdraw money from his accounts began tentatively. It didn't take long, though, for those calls to become routine. At first, he seemed shy when asking, but he had justified every request. No matter how many times I reminded him of his goals, he had an excuse, and he would ultimately remind the three of us that he would *"soon be making millions every year."*

The top partner I worked for started noticing these withdrawals and called me into his office. He suggested I sit down and speak to Joey directly, get the true version of what was going on. I called Joey immediately, and we agreed to meet for lunch. Joey chose a restaurant where I knew the appetizers alone would set me back more than an entire meal at a traditional chain.

As I approached his table, Joey stood to greet me, and I estimated his suit had to be well over $3,000, the watch another several thousand dollars. A bracelet on his other wrist glistened with diamonds. He wore high-end sunglasses and fine Italian shoes. I groaned inside. The ambitious, innocent farm boy from Ohio was gone. In his place was another overnight millionaire who had gotten caught up in the lifestyle.

The conversation over lunch started small. We talked about little things like family, how everyone back home was doing. He asked about my life, and once the appetizers were finished, I guided the conversation to the more pressing financial topic.

He said things were going well. I caught a report from the newspapers recently about an injury that sidelined him for a few weeks. He didn't mention it. He also didn't discuss his waning work ethic, how he wasn't always showing up on time, sometimes leaving before the final practices were over, and exhibiting some alarming signs.

He did talk enthusiastically about investing in a nightclub that, as he put it, was guaranteed. "I mean, John, you wouldn't believe how much money this thing is going to make. It's going to put my accounts back where they started … and then some. And in just a few months."

I fought to keep my eyes from rolling, or to sigh, or to make any other gestures that could be taken as an offense, but I had already heard this story play out a dozen times in my relatively short career.

Every time I tried to guide the conversation back to his career, he brought up another "incredible opportunity" that had miraculously presented itself to him.

"Another guy I met is an expert in property development," he said as his filet mignon was nearing its end. "He wants to build in some area that's highly restricted, not even zoned, but John, he has connections no one else has, which is why this is such an amazing opportunity.

"Oh, and this other guy is this up-and-coming fitness guru. Maybe you've heard of him. He's going to be opening a new center and a whole line of fitness products and apparel. I'm telling you, they want my endorsement, and this will absolutely put them over the top. It will set me up for new opportunities, some major endorsement deals in the next few years."

Listening to him, I was amazed at how deluded he had become. Joey honestly felt he was on the fast track to fame, stardom, and endless riches.

I didn't want to order dessert, but since the conversation was still moving, I held in there for the duration. I thought that if I could help him see the futility in this thinking, he might stop the bloodletting and seal up those accounts.

When I was finally able to turn the conversation toward those accounts, he said he knew he was draining them now, but they would be completely replenished, way beyond where they were at their peak. I reminded him those accounts never hit much beyond $1 million because he almost immediately started drawing against them.

"I understand," he said to me, "but you don't know these people like I do. These investments are legit. I mean, they even flew me out to Catalina on their helicopter!"

They dressed, acted, and rode around in vehicles that played right into the traditional part, and he bought it hook, line, and sinker. It was in that moment, dessert finished, the silverware resting neatly on fine china, that I knew this was a lost cause. There was nothing I or anyone else could say or do at this point that would convince him to stop.

I even asked about his baseball training, trying to draw his attention back to where his real value and financial future rested, but he didn't want to talk much about it. He said everything was fine and continued to push the conversation back to these business deals. He claimed the Dodgers were happy with his progress, but I knew better.

He mentioned his position coach wasn't using him to the best of his abilities, and that's when all the pieces clicked into place. I'd read similar comments in sports reports from professional baseball, basketball, and even football players who were sliding down out of their respective careers. They couldn't see the problems with their abilities and instead blamed diminishing stats on their coaches.

Now, Joey was doing the exact same thing. A lingering hamstring injury was a continual problem now, too, so he was in rehab (again). With a lack of focus, low workout effort, it was no wonder he couldn't heal and get back out on the field.

One thing was obvious, though, throughout the conversation. He never mentioned the Major Leagues. Not once. During our initial conversations, all he seemed to talk about was the Big Leagues. Now, it was nothing more than a footnote.

The Dodgers were losing interest in him. Fast. Joey was not progressing as they'd hoped. He was taking far too long to rehab this injury, and his mind wasn't on baseball anymore. It showed. He was a shooting star, burning bright in the first moments and quickly fading into darkness with no hope of getting back to his original form or potential. He had essentially given up that dream.

By the time we had sat down in that restaurant, the Dodgers had, too, already looking to downgrade or cut their losses for Joey "Baseball." Joey didn't seem to care. Everything was now about these amazing deals that would hit on all cylinders soon enough.

By the time we had sat down in that restaurant, the Dodgers had already been looking to downgrade or cut their losses for Joey "Baseball." Joey didn't seem to care. Everything was now about these amazing deals that would hit on all cylinders soon enough.

He was cut less than a year and a half later. I think the Dodgers organization shopped him around as long as they could, but his stock had plummeted. No other teams were interested.

By then, he had a little money left in the accounts we managed, but despite our best efforts to encourage him to leave it alone, he withdrew everything and went all-in with these other "investments." His need to keep up appearances ultimately crushed him and his life savings.

Joey got drawn into a life he thought was necessary, something he thought he honestly needed. Sadly, it wasn't him. It wasn't anything for him. It didn't fill any void or give him a sense of purpose. He got caught by *status*.

In the end, Joey walked away with nothing. All those investments that were "sure things" fizzled. Whether they were scams or the legitimate endeavors of entrepreneurs who simply blew the whole thing, I couldn't possibly know.

For a long time Joey held onto some measure of hope that one of those investments would finally pay out, but he never heard from any of those so-called partners again. They vanished like the wind using Joey's money to fund their lavish lifestyle. It was sad to watch.

Years later, I looked Joey up on Facebook, and he seemed to be okay. He was teaching and coaching baseball at his local high school in Ohio. His annual income was a far cry from what he'd had to invest at 18. If he works the next 30 years of his life, he won't earn close to what he would have made in just one year with a Major League contract. I will say, though, based on his photos, he seemed happy and content.

> **Money doesn't mean happiness; it's about staying true to who you are, to the friends and family who honestly care about you, and your principles.**

That's the thing; some people crash and burn and can never crawl back up. Others realize money doesn't mean happiness; it's about staying true to who you are, to the friends and family who honestly care about you, and your principles. He may have slipped away from those core values for a while, but held onto them in the end.

His baseball career could have been phenomenal, but the door of easy money, delusional investment opportunities, endless parties, and the need to play a part and be someone he wasn't crushed his dreams. Things could have been so different for Joey and for so many others who have faced the same temptations. It takes just one diversion to lose sight of your target and in an instant, you've struck out.

Trap Eight:
Strike Three ... You're OUT!

BELIEFS: I know what I'm doing; I'll make more money.

EXCUSES: "If I don't jump in now, I'll lose out on these opportunities and not look cool to my friends and family."

ACTIONS: Spending money like there's no tomorrow.

RESULTS: Strike three! You're now broke.

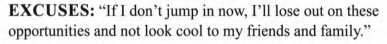

Kids are fascinated with the world around them. I love watching children discover life. There's a sense of awe and wonder that emanates from them and can be infectious. Watch a young child visit the beach for the first time, see the waves crashing around them and feel the cold water lap their feet and ankles. Listen to their giddiness as their toes dig into the sand.

It's a great reminder for each of us that life is special. Life is an amazing experience and yet we get so caught up in pursuing our careers and building our savings for retirement that sometimes we forget to take pleasure in the simple things it offers.

But when we graduate high school, we should be leaving that moniker of "kid" behind. We should be equipped with enough maturity, information, knowledge, and advice to handle adult-type situations.

Compared to the rest of history, modern American teenagers are poorly equipped to handle the everyday pressures of life, and it's tragic.

Less than 100 years ago, some American children were being pulled from school to help their parents on the farm, in a factory, in a dangerous mine, or on foreign soil shouldering a rifle for their country. They had no choice, but today many 18-, 19-, and even 25-years olds grudgingly take a job when their parents *finally* give them an ultimatum.

Abraham Lincoln didn't go to school. He only had a couple of books because his parents were so poor. After his mother passed away before he was 10, his childhood was devoted to doing whatever he could to help his father survive. He read those few books over and over, and that was what counted for his education until much later in life.

Today, our culture tends to coddle our children. We try to protect them from the world, the evils that surround us, and want them to enjoy these younger years for as long as possible. And somehow that has been bleeding into young adulthood, too.

Joey was the All-American kid from the Midwest who was drafted by the Los Angeles Dodgers. If there was ever a city that could contrast the countryside lifestyle he had in Ohio, Los Angeles was certainly it.

When he first contacted me, I was impressed by his focus. He was grounded and seemed mature for his age. In the Minor League, he was still grounded. He had a sincere and strong desire to work hard, remain humble, and focus on his goal. Sadly, all that quickly evaporated when he became immersed in a completely new lifestyle. The L.A. lifestyle. I could imagine his parents instilling in him this idea of personal responsibility, thinking about his future, and especially about his life after baseball, because very few truly make a long career of any professional sport.

But in major cities like Los Angeles, financial predators are relentless and temptations abound. They circle the young, the vulnerable. There are plenty of people who understand how to play the con game so well they appear as friends, as fellow sheep just trying to avoid the slaughter. In truth, they're ravenous wolves.

I know what it's like to have someone take my money and run. I once lent a good friend in this industry money. It was a considerable sum, and though he signed a formal contract, he never bothered to pay any of it back. He basically stole the money. You can know someone quite well, work with them for years, have their family over for dinners, and they can still burn you.

Joey soon shirked the responsibility of practicing and honing his craft in pursuit of the nightlife L.A. offered and the promise of "easy money."

He got a taste of what money could buy, and his *Belief* was that he could handle it just fine. Other athletes making millions upon millions of dollars were driving the kind of cars he only dreamt about back in Ohio. They were attending the parties and hobnobbing with celebrities, and they were bringing him along, exposing him to a life he had never really imagined he could enjoy – the life he saw on television.

Suddenly his decision to rely on me as his financial advisor caused him an internal dilemma. He wanted to do the right thing, but he needed the money to keep up with his new friends and his new persona. As he withdrew the money and as I attempted to calm him down and try to refocus his attention, he became more determined that he could handle the situation.

His *Excuse* became wanting to enjoy the good life now. Then he got turned around and focused on the wrong things. He bought into the idea that if he invested his money with certain people, they would parlay it into tens of millions of dollars. He bought into the idea that if he invested in a nightclub he would be the talk of the town, the one celebrities would all want to hang out with. He bought into the idea that this was where his future lay, not in baseball, especially when his production was down and injuries were up. The more he focused on things off the field, the more it affected his performance and his physical health.

His *Actions* involved spending money with no temperance. This was about impressing people back home, showing that he had made it on his own without baseball. All his life he had been told how great of an athlete he was. This was his way of showing his friends and family that he could do it without his right arm.

Joey never stopped thinking about his post-baseball life. He just began thinking about it too early and in the wrong way (before he really even played), and the *Result* was a clear strikeout – "caught looking," as baseball announcers are apt to say.

GETTING CAUGHT

Beliefs: I know what I'm doing; I'll make more money. We get comfortable in the idea that we're smart enough to handle our money, whether it comes over decades or overnight. Unfortunately, thanks to the failures of our education system, few of us are financially literate enough to handle money properly.

Excuses: "If I don't jump in now, I'll lose out on these opportunities and not look cool to my friends and family." Who wants to think about tomorrow when you can enjoy the fruits of your winnings now? This is one of the greatest challenges financial advisors face today: convincing people to delay gratification and instead focus on their future.

Actions: Spending money like there's no tomorrow. No matter how a person comes into money, when it's a vast financial windfall, they honestly think it's never going to end. They start spending, getting deeper into a hole, helping and sometimes bailing out friends and family, and they fail to keep track of where everything is going. It's blind spendthrift that can lead to ruin.

Results: Strike three! *You're now broke.* A brief list of familiar names of people or companies that have declared bankruptcy (as I mentioned in the beginning of this book): José Canseco, Stephen Baldwin, Leon Spinks, Mike Tyson, Larry King, MC Hammer, Willie Nelson, Gary Busey, Nicholas Cage, Henry Ford, JC Penney, Debbie Reynolds, Walt Disney, P.T. Barnum, Mark Twain ... do I really need to go on? It's all the same story.

How many children who start playing sports imagine they're about to hit the game-winning home run, score the winning touchdown, and win the championship? It's a fantasy so many of us have in our younger years. To this day, I still lose sleep over the tackles I missed, the plays I messed up on, and the opportunities on the field I let slip by.

Do we ever really let go of those fantasies?

Hitting a walk-off home run, especially in the seventh game of the World Series, would be quite an accomplishment. But championships are not won with one swing of the bat; they come at the expense of one little single, a bunt to advance the runners, and a sacrifice fly to deep centerfield.

The same holds true in our financial lives. If we can just remember that it's those small hits that win games, the season, and the championship, we can avoid the B.E.A.R. Trap when it springs up.

The best time to protect your money is when you have some

If you want financial success, a simple fact you must embrace is that the best time to protect your money is when you have some.

YOUR TURN

Let's take another look at your life. Keep things in perspective. Pull out your guidebook and complete Activity #11.

This is another opportunity to begin diving deep down to the roots and see how your beliefs are impacting your financial life.

CHAPTER 14

Reason Nine:
I Have an Amazing Idea!

There are plenty of people who feel as though their life is complete. They might not be making a great deal of money, but they've accomplished many of their goals, are content with what they have, and don't feel compelled to prove something to anyone. In modern society these individuals are becoming the exception rather than the rule.

Today there are growing numbers of people from all socioeconomic backgrounds who somehow feel what they have, what they're doing, what they *are* isn't enough. That desire for more can be positive and a great motivator to never stop growing and to live life to its fullest. It's a powerful mindset to have if you're looking to improve yourself and the life of others.

Personally, I've never been content with what I've accomplished, which is why I continue to push myself to pursue more in all aspects of my life. But, there's another side to this need for more and that's where danger lurks (that's where the B.E.A.R. Trap lingers).

This side can be attributed to ego, where the desire for more is based on external forces and rewards rather than internal fulfillment, or what I refer to as "psychological income." A major source of this ego-based need can be rooted in insecurity based on someone's upbringing, experiences, and failures.

This can be seen in people who have a strong need to constantly impress others – whether it's how often they exercise and work out, the car they drive, the size of their house, their circle of friends, their clothes, etc. Today, many people are becoming more and more susceptible to powerful marketing campaigns via social media and/or television. We are faced with a daily barrage of images and messages from celebrities and those ads are specifically designed to make people feel inferior or incomplete. We see our Facebook and Instagram friends posting about all of their successes in life. Suddenly, you feel you *must* have more success, more accomplishments, more wealth, better vacations, a nicer house, a better car, and so on.

People with millions upon millions of dollars and those who are scraping pennies together just to buy some food can suffer from the same temptations, those same desires to rush out and pursue an idea, believing it is the next "big thing."

We see products everywhere we turn, little mementos and gadgets that turn into "must haves" that – after a few minutes of use or enjoyment – will soon find a box that will be stuffed in the attic, in a storage container, or in the back of your closet. Eventually, these things are thrown away or sold at a garage sale for pennies on the dollar or simply dropped off at the nearest Goodwill.

Yet there are also amazing ideas that help alleviate pain, discomfort, give people a sense of hope, or fill a specific need. Technological innovations, ergonomics, mental health, miracle supplements, muscle enhancers, organizational tools, and so on. The list is as endless as the ideas … they never cease to keep coming at us!

Most of these ideas, though, take a small fortune (and, often, a small army) to bring to life. For every single product that hits the shelves in any type of store or online there are thousands upon thousands of others that fall away before coming to fruition.

And there are tens of thousands of people who have spent their life savings – even millions of dollars – trying to develop these ideas and bring them out to the public only to see them crash and burn.

Over the years, I've seen this countless times with people thinking they have the next great idea. With blinders on and no real business plan, they start spending wildly, wasting hundreds if not thousands of dollars on an idea they were convinced was going to be a huge success. Months, if not years later, they finally come to a variety of realizations including that the idea was a dud, they have no idea how to take it to market it, or they've run out of money. They get so focused on this idea and will not allow any objective analysis. They often view this "incredible" idea as their quick fix to solve their financial problems or gain status amongst their friends and loved ones.

It's not just ideas and products they dive into. There are tens of thousands of people who buy into affiliate marketing campaigns and MLM (multi-level marketing) companies with a dream of making *"thousands of dollars a week working just a few hours from home!"*

They are sold this promise of easy money selling products and/or services people *absolutely need*. They invest and start devoting time to it. In some cases, they quit their jobs to make time to focus on this new venture.

They fail to see the bigger picture, the endless hours, mistakes, and marketing methods that'll be necessary to make it work.

Whether it's selling other people's products or innovating one of their own, too many of these men and women dive in without a plan. It's like launching your body headfirst into water and having no idea whether it's deep or not.

Some might get lucky. Others could lose everything.

I once worked with a man in La Jolla, California who had made a literal fortune in the oil business and retired early. He felt a certain amount of guilt concerning his fortune, because everyone knew he had been at the right place at the right time and luck, rather than skill, was on his side. Having said that, he had been a driven and dedicated professional throughout his 20s and 30s and had worked hard. It wasn't long into retirement that he became restless.

That's a common danger that people with drive and ambition face when they walk away from the working world too young. They end up having too much time on their hands and begin losing their sense of purpose.

This man was truly set for life. But as we've seen time after time in these stories, there's no such thing as guaranteed financial security –

especially when you make poor decisions and refuse to acknowledge the problem before it's too late.

Having retired more than 5 years earlier, Zack slipped into a state of restlessness. In his mid-50s, he played tennis at their local country club, hit the links with friends, and sat on a few community boards, but he wasn't feeling fulfilled.

After several years, Zack grew tired of the routine, and felt a strong desire for more purpose in life. One afternoon, he and his wife were discussing technological innovations. In a moment of inspiration, Zack had an epiphany.

"This is going to change the world," he said.

That became his mantra whenever he discussed his idea with friends, colleagues, or anyone who would listen. He kept the details close to the vest; he was petrified somebody would steal the idea, create a prototype, patent it, and manufacture the technology before he could.

I had been his financial advisor for a number of years at this time, so it didn't come as any surprise when Zack filled me in on this idea one afternoon as I sat down with him to go over his financial affairs. The idea certainly did sound like a good one, but as I also relayed, it sounded more like a novelty than a necessity.

It was easy to tell there was no talking him down at that time, so I didn't feel it was my place or the right time to share my pessimism and mention the market for this type of product was likely small. Another key complication I recognized was that for this idea to work, it was going to require the cooperation of a variety of other companies. That's a hard nut to crack, especially in the technology sphere.

Having had no children, Zack came to see this idea as his baby. He had more than enough money to make this work, and no advice or counsel was going to deter him. I kept having to remind myself that he honestly believed this was going to change the world.

Maybe he's right, I thought. *What do I know?* I wasn't a product development expert and I know nothing about technology.

The one thing I did know was that there have been thousands if not millions of incredible ideas and "perfect" business opportunities that never panned out, that never led to financial freedom or success. In most cases, those entrepreneurial ideas, product innovations, and small to midsize businesses used up a lot of money and failed within the first five years.

One thing I've learned through all these years as I've seen people strive for success is that determination is essential. People often pursue something because "it's their passion" and they've been told that's the way to go, but it doesn't equal success. There are plenty of "passionate" people on Shark Tank, American Idol, and a seemingly endless stream of reality TV contestants pursuing their passions, and when they are told they're no good, they're devastated.

Success in business *starts* by devoting yourself to something, gaining experience, and then when you have an idea, to figure out a way to do it better, differently, cheaper (fill in the blank here) to set yourself apart from the competition. Of course, you need a product or service with a real, sustainable market.

> **Success in business *starts* by devoting yourself to something, gaining experience, and then when you have an idea, to figure out a way to do it better, differently, cheaper to set yourself apart from the competition.**

Ignore the market and you're rolling the dice. You'd have better odds heading to Vegas to play craps if that's the approach.

I didn't get that sense from him. His motivation seemed to stem from it being *his brilliant idea*. It came across as more about ego and proving something to the world.

I recommended a friend to Zack who did graphic design and development. She was good at her job and was reasonable with her rates. Zack wanted nothing to do with that; this was a person who believed that paying top dollar for something meant he was getting the best. He actively sought out designers who were charging the most exorbitant rates. He needed a designer from New York because that's where only the best come from. In all honesty, what those "experts" were creating was really no better and barely any different from what my contact and hundreds of others were doing for a much lower fee.

I introduced him to a book I thoroughly enjoyed called *The Lean Start-Up*. It's one of the best entrepreneurial books I've read on launching a new business. It's based on the premise that most startups fail, but many of those failures are preventable. It hits on the need to be lean and learn what customers want at the early stages and relies on a concept called "validated learning" where you test ideas so you can immediately adapt rather than spending every last dime on getting your product to market only to learn it's a product no one wanted.

He politely thanked me for the suggestion, but his facial expressions proved he wanted nothing to do with this book. He knew his product and was convinced it would be a success. Spending money on high end service providers and experts was Zack's way of saying he was going big.

He focused on the most expensive designers, technology specialists, engineers, and other providers. After two years, he finally developed a simple prototype. This was after spending over one hundred thousand dollars on international and domestic patents and thousands more on other legal documents. However, Zack tested the product only among a few close, trusted friends. That circle of friends wasn't exactly the kind that would be open and honest; they'd be more concerned about not alienating themselves from their inner circle or being dismissed from it altogether. So this product essentially had zero market testing.

I watched his accounts dwindle. Tens of thousands of dollars would simply vanish almost on a daily basis. I mentioned these issues, that he was depleting some of his savings and even drawing on some of his investments to fund this endeavor, but as I've learned through these many years, sometimes all you can do is manage what you're hired to do the best you can while remembering your clients are in control. It's their money, not yours.

I couldn't stop him, and until he was pushing against the brink of future bankruptcy or other serious issues, I had to stay the course, even though I recognized this was a train speeding recklessly toward a hard turn.

Instead of slowing down, he ramped it up. He took his new business endeavor and made it official, opening up an office and hiring a number of staff. Instead of outsourcing to freelance designers and specialists, he brought staff on board with full benefits and great pay. He never considered what these niche-oriented experts would do for him once their initial projects were completed.

Of course, this new office had to have the best of everything. That meant spending top dollar for the best office computer systems, networks, desks, high-end business cards, and even ergonomic chairs. The office had more than a dozen Aeron office chairs – they were incredibly popular during the dot-com era, valued at about $1,000 *each*. The office had to look as though the company was successful already. I heard from a mutual acquaintance that Zack had invited him and his wife over. "You have to see this office," Zack had said.

The amount of money I saw pouring out of his accounts was disturbing. Yet every effort I made to stem the bleeding was met with resistance. One afternoon over the phone I was told – in no uncertain terms – to "just drop it."

So I did.

It was obvious to more than a few others who understood the situation that Zack didn't have a clue what he was doing. He had made good investments in the oil industry, but as a technology entrepreneur he was out of his element. To make up for his lack of experience and knowledge, he simply threw more money at everything.

His ego was in too deep to turn around now. If he stopped, what would his friends think? He could under no uncertain terms let his friends think he failed. That was *his* mentality.

After several years running at this pace, Zack finally realized this idea was never going to take off. Too many obstacles, too many setbacks, too many failed promises by others and too many unanswered phone calls by those he was trying to work with and sell to. It was a burden too big to carry any further.

Zack's idea was a good one but only for a narrow segment of the population. A tiny niche. A perfect idea for a hobby. It simply didn't get off the ground because Zack did not have any clue how to get it in front of the right people, test it properly, objectively see its flaws, and help it evolve.

That's the thing about ideas: they can strike at just about any time and can appear completely polished, perfect, and absolutely the "next big thing," but in many cases they go through transitions. They evolve. The finished product is often completely different from the original idea. Sometimes they're basically the same, but between design, refinement, testing, and all the other work that goes into developing truly successful products and services, change is almost inevitable.

> **That's the thing about ideas ... The finished product is often completely different from the original idea.**

Shark Tank is a U.S. television reality program where entrepreneurs present their innovations to multi-millionaire investors (incredibly successful business men and women) who decide if they like it and want to invest in it. Few who present on this show get any deals, but even among those who do find investment, more often than not it fizzles and fails.

And that's with the support of shrewd, experienced business professionals backing them up!

All told, Zack dumped more than $4.5 million into this project and essentially lost it all. Yes, he had his own business. He had a team of employees. He had the most impressive office furniture. It all looked successful from the outside, but as with so many things where image is king, it was shallow and hollow on the inside.

No, Zack didn't go broke. He didn't have to declare bankruptcy, but those reckless years definitely hurt his financial situation. He eventually had to sell the 7,000-square-foot house he had been living in and downsize. He could no longer afford to stay where he was.

He was lucky – one of the few who can say that, having had so much wealth and recklessly spending a significant portion of it.

Ideas are fickle and fleeting and plentiful. The desire to be thought of as successful, to measure one's self-worth by what others think is a common problem that devastates not just the rich but the middle class and, sometimes, the poor.

The dangling promise of riches and success can drive anyone to devote their precious time and whatever financial resources they have into pursuing it, even in the face of warnings and a complete lack of understanding about market needs.

Even to financial ruin.

There are a bastion of scams running that urge people to "protect their ideas," talking about patents and risk of losing those ideas, and so on. Almost all of these are borderline fraudulent and I recommend everyone to steer clear of them at all cost.

Pursuing an entrepreneurial vision is wonderful. It's the catalyst that drives economies and businesses. However, you need to temper enthusiasm and have a clear mission, well-defined goals, a thorough business plan, and a detailed budget in place before diving down into those shark infested waters.

Zack didn't, but he was lucky. He is the exception to the rule.

THE BREAKDOWN

Trap Nine:
The Grass is Always Greener

BELIEFS: I have a brilliant idea. I want people to see me as accomplished.

EXCUSES: "The more we spend on this idea, the more we're going to make."

ACTIONS: Throwing money on an idea with little thought or analysis. Focusing on image instead of substance.

RESULTS: Failed business and hampered financial future.

Make $1,000 in just four hours a week!
Do you have an idea for an awesome new product?
This incredible health supplement can also bring you financial independence!
Patent that amazing idea before somebody else does!

I want you to pay attention to something. For the rest of this day and throughout tomorrow, just pay attention to the number of ads your eyes see. You don't need to read them or even *look* at them, but whether in your peripheral or in your face, pay attention.

We are bombarded by slick marketing campaigns, empty promises, and a host of ads for food, cars, prescription medications, vacations, business opportunities, and much more. In fact, the average American is exposed to more than 4,000 advertisements every day.

Sounds ridiculous, doesn't it?

Pay attention.

Visit a website, even a basic news organization to simply check on what's happening in the world and mark down how many ads – video, single-line, image, etc. – you see. What about your email? How much junk do you get daily?

You may barely pay attention to 20, notice fewer than 10, and remember 3 or 4. But of those 4,000 ads, a majority of them are in fact sneaking into your subconscious and playing dirty tricks in your mind.

They are manipulating you, your thoughts, and your *Beliefs*.

Marketing campaigns have tens of thousands, even millions of dollars poured into them. The higher quality, more expensive campaigns often rely on intensive and extensive research to hit the emotional triggers as powerfully as possible.

That's why, when you see an ad or a simple sentence promising great reward with little investment or risk, it hits home.

That's what we want.

We want to win the lottery. We think sudden riches will take care of our problems. We'll no longer have to wake up at the crack of dawn, peeling our eyes open, letting the cold shower dribble over our skin to get the blood flowing, and drag our car through the nightmare of rush-hour traffic just to squeeze into our cubicle, punch in our required eight hours of mindless work, and slog home.

Even though most people will admit they're happy with their job, their life, or their future prospects, if given an opportunity to pursue greater riches, a lesser workload, or a more rewarding future, they'll take it without a second thought.

A computer virus struck a major company a number of years ago. It was called the Pink Slip virus, and its delivery method was ingenious. It came in the form of a simple email with a subject line to the effect of "Sick of Your Job?" Of course, there have been numerous parodies and other advertisements that took advantage of this example, but it was a real virus that hit, and hit hard.

Most of the employees at this particular company opened that email at work and unleashed the virus into their closed network. It wreaked havoc. It cost the company millions of dollars, but it highlighted a glaring yet simple reality. Even people with decent pay, good benefits, and job security are often looking for a better opportunity.

They're just not happy.

So we find promises of making thousands of dollars every week (putting in only a few hours of our time) appealing. We regularly see boasts about incredible health supplements practically guaranteeing users will lose weight, overcome devastating diseases that have stumped medical professionals and researchers for years, and even invigorate the brain and increase memory retention. Oh, and if you jump in and start selling these products, it's "practically guaranteed" that you'll have financial independence in a matter of weeks, if not days!

Now, back to our regularly scheduled reality.

Far too many of us seek to escape reality within these promises. *The grass is always greener on the other side of the fence*.

> **The grass is always greener on the other side of the fence.**

This adage remains true to this day. It basically means no matter what you have, no matter the size of the house you might own or are renting, the car you drive, the vacations you take, how much money you've saved, the kind of smartphones or tablets you have, the size of your TV, etc. … it all seems to pale in comparison to what somebody else has. And though we understand that warning, we continue looking for something better.

Blend that into the social media phenomenon that is Facebook, Twitter,

Instagram, Pinterest, and SnapChat, and you have a perfect storm that's been brewing for years. Many people who post regularly on social media are either making things up or **only** posting the things they want other people to see.

They are, in essence, creating a false reality for themselves and others. Like Zack, they are seeking outward recognition and accolades from people they know and sometimes strangers to help them feel as though they matter, as though their life is worth something.

While not many people are actually going to quit their full-time job and jump into some opportunity that promises $2,000 or even $5,000 per week with little effort, it does happen. People may lose focus at their current job and begin spending more of their energy trying to get this new opportunity off the ground.

They see the boasts, the testimonials from all those successful entrepreneurs who took the chance and are now basking in fun and sun at the beach, traveling the world at their leisure, and letting the money simply flow into their accounts. Those testimonials are either complete fiction or represent only those who got in on the ground floor (way, way back in the beginning of the business).

Why do people buy into these ideas? Why do they fall for these empty promises?

Some people have a tendency to jump at a new idea hoping to earn the kind of money they either want or feel they deserve. Or they want family or friends to see them as successful, as an entrepreneur who is now, finally, making it.

Please, do not misunderstand the point of this story or problematic belief system. I am in no way saying that entrepreneurship or pursuing ideas and developing them into products or services to build a business is a bad idea.

In fact, I believe the opposite to be true.

I believe this country is built on the fabric of ingenuity, innovation, and an entrepreneurial spirit. What I do warn about, though, is the motivation that drives somebody to get invested in any business venture – be it joining a multi-level marketing company, affiliate marketing, buying into a franchise, developing a product from an idea, or even starting their own company.

A person motivated by money and money alone (or at least with money being the highest priority) runs a serious risk of going broke, having to file bankruptcy, or being otherwise financially devastated.

Why?

As we saw with Zack, it's often difficult to convince somebody who has dollar signs in their eyes or is seeking external recognition and accolades to put the brakes on and evaluate the situation honestly. He was more concerned with someone stealing his idea than actually nurturing it, getting advice, and listening to sound counsel.

In order to build a successful business or bring a product to fruition, it requires investment. Yes, it does require financial investment. It also requires time and dedication. But it also demands sound judgment, a solid plan, measurable goals and deadlines, and a long-term expectation of return or escape.

Jumping into some endeavor without any concrete limit to what you may spend on it, how much time you may devote to it before you start receiving any reward, or any way out for your personal protection is asking for trouble.

In over 25 years of working with people as a financial advisor, I've met with thousands of men and women from all walks of life and across almost the entire spectrum of wealth statuses. Many of them have seemed to possess an insatiable desire to pour good money into what they view as opportunities – even if all the research points to something being a bad investment – and it's always with the expectation of getting a lot more money back. Over the years I've had countless phone calls from clients asking me to check out some obscure stock because they were interested in making an investment simply because they overheard that this company was about to skyrocket.

Most of these people really have no clue what they're doing or investing in. They spend little to no time studying the company, the product or the service they offer, or how it may be received by the consumer public. They buy into the marketing. They buy the promises. They buy the expectation.

When you look at every failed opportunity and all the billions of dollars that have been thrown away by the rich on these perceived golden opportunities, it would have been better for them to simply donate that money to worthy charities that take care of animals, clothe children, feed the hungry, promote the arts, or whatever happens to be important to that individual.

This isn't about social justice; I'm simply attempting to highlight that there is great value in doing good and putting your money to work for something bigger than yourself, or at the very least to *respect what you do earn enough to be careful with where you put it*. In my experience, without that mindset, you are at greater odds of throwing your money away.

> **Respect what you do earn enough to be careful with where you put it**

Why is that?

For every individual, the answer may be different. Overall, though, it seems to boil down to a desire to fill a void. We don't feel satisfied with what we are or have. We look outward rather than inward.

The grass *always* seems greener elsewhere.

And that's where the trouble starts.

We want to feel good. It's why we pursue the finer clothing, enjoy the fancier restaurants when we can afford it, or go to the types of movies we enjoy.

Our *Belief* is that it will make us happier.

It's one of the reasons so many people living paycheck to paycheck pay ridiculous amounts of money for their smartphones. They have the iPhone or Galaxy that might cost them $1,000 for the device, $120 a month for the service. They pay another $160 a month for cable and internet, subscribe to Netflix and Amazon Prime, join the high end health club, eat out on a regular basis at expensive restaurants, only buy expensive wines because they "taste better." I could go on and on and I don't mean to judge – I'm simply highlighting our problems as a society, because we're all in this together.

Doing these things *feels* good, right?

Add up every dollar you spend in a month for which there is a far cheaper alternative, and you'll likely be stunned at the total wasted on these fleeting things.

Yet we cling to these beliefs that we deserve the better things because we've been convinced they'll make us happier and we build *Excuses* to justify our continued purchases.

Our *Actions* end up supporting our excuses and harden our beliefs. Zack certainly filled that bill to the proverbial T. He needed to look the part so he could be deemed a "legitimate" businessman. His actions belied his flawed beliefs.

Now, if Zack had invested properly in that idea he had, he would have discovered the narrow market for it. That could have saved him millions of dollars. It could have led him to a different idea or to tinkering with his main product to move it into a more lucrative market. We don't know. We'll never know.

The *Results* become clear: financial loss, failure, and potential ruin.

GETTING CAUGHT

Beliefs: I have a brilliant idea. I want people to see me as accomplished. Zack needed people to believe he had it all together. One look at his spending for office supplies and the comments he made as to his top priorities highlights this deficient mode of thinking.

Excuses: "The more I spend on this idea, the more I'm going to make." Since Zack had already found success in one industry, it made sense he could catch lightning in a bottle again. He failed to understand there were major differences between one field and the other.

Actions: Throwing money on an idea with little thought or analysis. Focusing on image instead of substance. His insatiable desire to be seen as a success came before actual success. It held the highest priority for him.

 Results: Failed business and hampered financial future. Zack was lucky to have walked away with something. He needed to downgrade his home and other essentials, but he still didn't need to worry about finances for the rest of his lif. It was close … many others are not as fortunate.

What makes for a successful life? Every person has to come up with the answer to this question themselves, but if you're constantly looking to your friends through the social media lens, if you look to celebrities and what they want everyone else to see, or you get caught up in the idea a new phone, new computer, new car, or new house is going to *finally* bring you happiness, you will forever be chasing an elusive dream and never find happiness.

Some people who report being the happiest are often the ones who go home at the end of the day smelling to high heaven with dirt or grease or oil under their fingernails. They've found contentment in their family, in what they can afford, and don't believe there's a need for more. Sure, they'd take a winning lottery ticket if it was handed to them, but they may not chase after the next materialistic craze because they can't afford it and it isn't important to them.

No one gets out of this life alive, and we don't get to take a single penny with us to the other side. Everything we create, everything we earn, stays.

In most business endeavors and financial opportunities, *if it sounds too good to be true, it usually is.* If you're constantly measuring your life against the backdrop of friends, families, superstars, coworkers, or people you see passing on the street, you'll never be happy.

You could become the CEO of your company, earn tens of millions of dollars every single year, and be content for a while, happy to be able to buy whatever you want, travel wherever you wish, and not worry about finances ever again, but one day you will wake up, look around, and like Zack, feel something is missing.

I climbed the corporate ladder and got pretty close to the top. The people I reported to were all worth well over $25 million. The one thing that was clearly noticeable was how unhappy and dissatisfied they were with their overall life. Deep down they were not happy people, not pleasant people, not good people. They all wanted more and were willing to do anything to get more.

If you have an innovative idea, celebrate. If you desire to invest in a new business opportunity, great. Simply take your time, go slow, evaluate all the facts, and don't lean on your emotions when they are most intense (e.g. when you're stressed, or swept up in the excitement). Also, *set your escape terms.*

Ignore the promises of riches. Determine if this opportunity is in line with your true purpose in life or is this simply about the money? Evaluate your abilities objectively and factually and not with your feelings. Ask for advice from people who have done what you're attempting to do and get a clear idea if this is something you are capable of doing. Take your time evaluating all the aspects of this endeavor or new product. Read *The Lean Startup*! Even if this is a part-time business opportunity, understand you might have to invest an average of 20 or more hours every single week for years before it becomes truly successful.

Is that something you're willing to do?

It's easy to say yes, but have you kept up other commitments? Do you go to the gym consistently? Have you stuck with other promises you've made to yourself or friends or family?

How have those New Year's resolutions gone in the past?

The reason I feel so strongly on this topic is that I've seen the immense harm that has come to so many wonderful people because they dove into things without vetting all the details. They wasted their life savings and even drove themselves and their family into bankruptcy.

If you think the grass looks greener now, just imagine how everything would look if you were completely broke, busted, or even homeless.

I'm not trying to be a killjoy. I am absolutely not trying to discourage you from pursuing dreams, investments, or business opportunities.

I am simply cautioning against jumping in without looking. Have a plan. Have measurable goals. Have expectations. And have a way *out.*

Do it all for the *right* reasons.

Protect yourself, your finances, and your family.

When people come to me for advice on various business endeavors or investments, I often recommend one book or another for them to read. I've yet to meet anyone who has actually read *any* of them. It doesn't matter what book; it's always something I feel can bring them value and help them with their upcoming effort. Yet if somebody is not willing to take the advice of an experienced financial advisor and read a simple book, what are they doing? I could recommend a podcast or a video. They never get watched. People say, "That's a good idea. I'll get right on that." But they never do.

No one ever seems to genuinely want to do the work. Yet everyone wants the magic diet busting pill, health supplement, or get-rich-quick scheme.

The grass is *not* always greener. If you're pursuing what you love, the reward is already there. If you're not, if you're constantly seeking bigger, better, faster, sleeker … what fertilizer is there in that?

Your grass, no matter how long it grows, will never get green enough.

 YOUR TURN

Let's take another look at your life. Keep things in perspective. Pull out your guidebook and complete Activity #12.

This is another opportunity to begin diving deep down to the roots and see how your beliefs are impacting your financial life.

CHAPTER 15

Reason Ten:
My Company Will
Take Care of Me

Luke and Sue were living a good life. They had moved to San Diego in the late 1990s for a promotion, and as a high-level executive with a major corporation, Luke was pulling in nearly half a million dollars per year.

When they first moved to San Diego, Sue had this idea of buying a couple of oceanfront properties. They were convinced it was a great time to do so, considering their location and future potential. To do so, Luke and Sue over-leveraged to buy two: one for themselves and one as a rental. It wasn't more than a year later they grew tired of condo living and they once again borrowed heavily to buy a stunning oceanfront home. They weren't willing to let go of the first condo, even with this new home. They saw it as an asset, despite the fact they didn't rent it out. They were convinced it was something that would invariably increase in value over time.

I initially met Luke and Sue through a mutual friend. They had so much money coming in they wanted to know the best thing to do with all that extra cash.

They immediately made an impression on me. Luke was smart, easygoing, and fun to be around. Sue was a wonderful woman with a penchant for the finer things. Her entire personality was larger than life. That first visit with Luke and Sue was a pleasant one – getting to know them, their lives, his work, their goals, their questions, and, most importantly, how they viewed money and their wealth.

Over the next few years, I would become much more familiar with these two. For a couple who wanted to live like they were rich (which they were), they hit the mark. Of course, living rich means spending rich and they were spending almost as fast as the money was pouring in. That's not an easy thing to do when you earn more than $42,000 per month!

I did caution them early on to be aware of their spending habits, but they weren't concerned. Luke worked for a major corporation, one with an upward growth trajectory, and he was sitting on what would eventually be a solid pension and a hefty amount of company employee stock options (ESOP).

Like so many others who come into money, they wanted a "balanced" portfolio, as they called it. This would be the bread-and-butter portfolio for most portfolio managers. It sure seemed as though they understood they should be reserved to some degree and have a diversified portfolio.

Their finances ran along smoothly for a number of years. But despite my efforts to help them understand the risks of having their mortgages and other expenses stretch their finances too thin, they continued to brush off my concerns.

We shifted once again to the topic of their retirement when I stopped by their house for a visit. Retirement is always one of the first things I discuss with clients, and it's one of the most important, so we inevitably come back to it again and again.

"What do you mean?" Sue asked. "You're taking care of our portfolio."

"A small percentage," I replied.

She looked around. "We've got this place. And the two condos."

"And how much of either is actually paid off?"

This brought a cloud over her demeanor.

"By the time we retire, they'll both be paid off, and we've got the condo, and our investments, Luke's pension, and company stock," she said. "By the way, what are our current returns?" She wasn't asking. She was taking a jab at me.

It was nearing the new millennium, and that meant people investing in stocks were fully immersed in the technology boom. Sue was paying attention to some things, usually the stories of men and women who were overnight millionaires because they'd bought into the right companies at the right time. She was itching to dump a load of cash into these stocks, too.

I squared my shoulders. "Good enough so you'll never have to worry about money in your Golden Years."

She snickered and *pshaw*ed me. "What about this?" she asked as she produced a newspaper clipping of a local man who had just cashed out over $2 million from a relatively small investment in an up-and-coming tech company.

"It was a good bet," I said honestly. "But that's all it is. A gamble."

Luke decided to chime in. "You've done a risk assessment on us, John."

"Yes, I did. And you both came back as moderate to conservative investors. You're being smart and building a solid portfolio for retirement."

"Aren't we missing out here?"

I studied them. They sat shoulder to shoulder across their gorgeous $10,000 mahogany dining room table, an exquisite China cabinet stocked with expensive decorative pieces, silver-plated picture frames, and a few tokens of their wedding day. They were a solid couple, completely in love and possessing a relationship I could only hope to have one day.

Yet they were also teaming up on me. They were addicted to the money, and they understood something was happening in the trading world that was unprecedented. They wanted in.

"I don't think so," I said cautiously. "You understand that the stock market isn't meant to make people millionaires overnight. It's not a casino."

"Yeah, but the World Wide Web is the in thing," Luke said. "It's the wave of the future!"

"That may be – "

"We don't want to look back in 10 years kicking ourselves because we didn't get in on the ground floor," said Sue.

There were so many things I wanted to say, but their minds were made up. They weren't looking for *advice*; they were seeking *confirmation*. I wasn't going to give it to them.

By this time, people were trading by themselves. They didn't need brokers and agencies. They could sign up online and take care of their buys and sells on their own.

I steeled my resolve and said, "I'm a financial advisor. That's what I'm paid to do. In my experience, in all my studies, and in the conversations I have with colleagues – some far more experienced than me – one thing is clear: this thing won't last. It can't."

"Exactly," Sue said. "Which is why we need to do this now."

"And what happens if … if you lose everything?"

She scoffed.

Luke seemed more tempered but still fully invested in the idea of buying tech stocks. "We won't. Don't you see, John? This is a no-lose situation. Besides," he added. "My company is solid. The bulk of our assets are in shares of stock in my company's ESOP, my company pension, and my income, which I'm certain will get even bigger. We're set for life."

"You're leveraged beyond your income," I told them. "Your debts outpace your income."

They both waved me off with a smile. "That's temporary. Everyone who buys real estate goes through that. Soon we'll be paying more on the principal and we'll have more equity."

I was going to remind them they currently had no equity on any of their properties but decided to hold off. This conversation was leading to one familiar destination.

"I implore you both to stay the course. You've been doing well. Your portfolio is strong, diversified, and built to hold up against almost every economic uncertainty."

I then suggested, they open a small account and play with it for a while.

"John," Sue said in her soft, compassionate voice. "This is something we've been discussing with each other for a while. We want to do this."

Luke took over. "If you can't get on board, it's okay. We appreciate what you've done for us. But we want to get in now, while it's fresh and nowhere to go but up."

It's times like that when I feel my heart sink, when all my effort to help a client ignites and burns through like chaff. They could be right, they could dump a few hundred thousand dollars in cash into tech stocks, ride the wave, and retire with tens of millions in their bank accounts. But there was something wrong with the market.

Stocks are meant to help companies grow and expand and to help investors build their wealth along with those companies. Yet many of these tech companies were startups. They were simply ideas. They had no real wealth, few had any measurable history upon which to base reasonable investment decisions, and only a handful actually produced anything of lasting value. The entire tech stock craze had the look and feel of a new casino game, designed to play to the favor of the gambler at first, giving just enough away to lure them in – but soon that door would slam shut, and the house always wins in the end.

This wasn't my first rodeo with the dot-com boom, as you've already read earlier with Rick and Mimi.

Although our professional relationship ended around June of 1999, I would still see Luke from time to time in various business circles and we would always have a nice chat. Sue took their investments and moved everything – including the bulk of their cash savings – to "do-it-yourself" financial institutions. She had become the expert and managed all their new investments.

While many of my colleagues and I could see the writing on the wall that things were about to dramatically change, none of us anticipated just how fast and how hard the crash would be.

The dot-com bust hit like a freight train carrying hundreds of cars. Anyone (and I mean **anyone**) who was still invested when it hit was done. There was nothing left.

These high-flying tech companies were not measured by their revenue or profits, but by their burn rate – the rate at which they burned through their investment capital. Far too many companies and their executives were convicted of fraud for misusing shareholder money. The U.S. Securities and Exchange Commission even levied massive fines against major reputable financial firms for misleading investors.

This dot-com bust didn't just wipe out these start-ups, it took everything down with them, including the big boys who actually had a viable business model. Some well-known companies managed to survive, including Cisco, Dell, Amazon, Qualcomm, and Priceline, but that was after dropping upwards of 90% in stock value. It was a brutal time for everyone.

Luke and Sue had been so gung-ho about investing in these tech stocks that they would have been like most people at that time: *holding on until it was far too late.* I could only imagine the devastating losses they had experienced.

Fortunately, Luke still had his job. At least, for a while.

Just when you thought things couldn't get any worse, they did. And like the dot-com bust, no one anticipated this cataclysmic event to occur. The world witnessed the most powerful, devastating terrorist attack unfold on live television.

What appeared to be just another Tuesday, several months after the dot-com bust, at 8:45 in the morning on the East Coast, a commercial passenger jet plowed into the north tower of the World Trade Center in New York City. That first strike on 9/11 was the beginning of what quickly turned into a colossal change for the country, the world, and Luke and Sue.

Luke was a high-powered executive for a major fortune 500 company that was directly affected by these attacks. In the aftermath – grounded flights, stranded passengers, and people suddenly afraid to travel or spend money – numerous industries were impacted.

Luke's job and the entire Southwest region of his company were suddenly considered expendable. His region would be overseen from headquarters. At 58, he was facing the prospect of losing his job or relocating. Neither Luke nor Sue had any desire to move, but finding another job with the same salary was going to be difficult.

Luke was clinging to the idea that his salary would continue and his pension and company stock would be enough to take care of them. Sadly, the ESOP was gone. It had perished as the company went into bankruptcy and the shares collapsed into dust. The company shares he owned were suddenly worthless as were the bulk of their assets. Before long, the ESOP was completely dissolved while the company struggled to stay alive.

I met Luke for coffee one morning and was taken aback by the difference in his appearance. He was stressed and it showed along every line on his face, in the sunken shoulders, and in the constant jittering of his hands. He had lost almost every extra penny from the dot-com bust and he wasn't prepared for the bad news that continued pounding down on his life.

"It's like a bad dream," he said. "And I just can't wake up from it."

"What are you and Sue doing now?"

He looked at me, a question in his eyes. His fingers played around the edges of his coffee mug, but he wasn't sipping it, only twirling it around. "What do you mean?"

"I mean, have you and Sue taken the steps you need in order to stop the bleeding? What are you doing to protect what you have?"

He didn't understand. "I don't get what you're saying. We're still okay."

No, they weren't.

Despite everything that had happened, despite everything they'd already lost and what was happening with a company he'd worked for all these years, despite the threats to his pension and his employment, they couldn't and wouldn't change their habits.

Although it was long overdue, there had never been a more critical time to make serious changes: to cut their spending, curtail the lavish lifestyle, trim their debts by selling one or both of their oceanfront properties, move back to the original condo, and start pumping their remaining (and freed cash from the sale of those houses) into solid, comfortable, and safe investments for their future. It wasn't too late. Though what they could earn by retirement was dramatically reduced now, these changes would be far better than having to scrape by working two jobs each through their 70s.

That afternoon was the last time Luke contacted me. Luke needed someone to be angry at and I was convenient. How dare I imply that their past decisions and current lifestyle had anything to do with their predicament! But that was never what I implied. I did, however, try to highlight that current decisions could be lifesavers down the road.

Less than a year later, Luke's position was terminated. To this day I'm not sure where he ended up or if he managed to get back on his feet. And to add to this perfect storm, just a few short years later I read in the news how the courts had given Luke's company permission to terminate its pensions, setting off one of the largest pension defaults in U.S. history.

The bottom line is Luke and Sue lost most if not all of their money. They had to start over.

This is a pattern that's starting to develop more frequently as pensions simply run out of money. Whether it's private or government funded, no pension is as secure as people prefer to believe. I don't care what the pension contract, agreement, or state constitution says, if there's no money to pay out, then there's no money to pay out. Period.

Luke and Sue made a classic mistake and relied primarily on their company to take care of them. They banked on future income instead of prudently managing their expenses and safely investing the difference because they felt nothing could go wrong. They trusted in the wrong things and held onto this outdated philosophy that the company he worked for would take care of them to the end.

No one could have anticipated the terror attacks that changed the world and that ultimately altered the future for the company, but that's the thing: there are forces beyond anyone's control that can impact anyone's future, no matter how wealthy they are. Salaries, pensions, and other company benefit plans are great, but not for putting *all* of your faith into them.

Trap Ten:
Living in the Bubble

BELIEFS: My company will take care of me.

EXCUSES: "As long as I have my job, I'll be just fine."

ACTIONS: Not planning for the "what-if" scenarios. Taking unnecessary risks, thinking nothing can go wrong.

RESULTS: Realizing that perfect storms do occur and discovering too late that everything you counted on could very well be an illusion.

We have a tendency to live in the moment and assume everything is going to be the same come next week, next month, and next year. We're driven to be successful at our jobs, climbing the proverbial ladder, and when we establish ourselves within the structure, we never look back. There's no need.

I once heard a close and trusted mentor tell me when high school was finally coming to an end that I should "find a good company with a pension to work for because they'll take care of you for life." I already sensed that wasn't the case. I'd seen and heard about layoffs at major corporations for years. IBM, General Foods, Ford, GM, and so many others were notorious for trimming staff when the economy shrank.

This mentor didn't want to hear it. He had worked most of his career in a different culture. The day of companies truly dedicating themselves to their employees was slipping into the tapestry of the past.

In the years since, I've come across far too many people who still cling to these notions. Despite economic facts, growth or contraction, debt and unfunded obligations, or other serious signs of potential problems, they take an "it-won't-happen-to-me" approach to life and simply count on the company they've been with for however many years.

By the time Luke and Sue entered my life, I had become a strong proponent of *not* putting all your faith in the future success of any company for which you worked or the pension it promised. Even by this time, I knew the importance of diversifying my income and my assets.

Luke and Sue were so focused on acquiring real estate, high flying stocks, and expensive possessions, which they could do at the time because of his income and perceived safety of his company, that they never envisioned anything changing. They had a *Belief* that his company was invincible, and he would have his job until retirement, so everything would work out as planned.

As we've all seen, even the strongest companies can collapse within a few short years and – even if they don't go bankrupt – they'll likely shed a significant percentage of their workforce, at least for a while. On top of that, people who get into the habit of holding onto property they can't afford, simply hoping and assuming they will appreciate in value, are most likely going to continue with that habit of purchasing more and more, digging themselves deeper and deeper into debt.

It's this belief that if you have more, you're worth more. It's this belief that if you simply buy more real estate, any real estate, you are wealthier. People discount the fact that those properties are actually leveraged by the bank, owned by the financial lender, at least until the note or mortgage is *fully* paid off. As Robert Kiyosaki has said repeatedly to much displeasure,

Your property is not an asset unless it produces positive cash flow. I couldn't agree more.

Neither Luke nor Sue were concerned about the distant future. Their belief system was set up in the current-rewards-based mentality. They had saved, they had worked hard, and now they were reaping the rewards of that effort. Why shouldn't they enjoy what they now had?

> **Your property is not an asset unless it produces positive cash flow.**

There's nothing wrong with enjoying money when you're earning it. There's nothing wrong with going on vacation, owning a nice house, having a vacation home, or even purchasing a property for rental purposes. However, when your primary residence is far from being paid off and you're living above your means, you will have a major problem, especially in the event something changes with your primary source of income.

Getting stuck in a belief that there won't be a change to your position leads to the *Excuse* that you can take a risk and it won't hurt. It leads to the excuse you don't need sound financial advice because you can always save later. It leads to the excuse that someone or something else will take care of you.

So many people measure their future income based on their current revenue. In other words, a person making $150,000 a year working for a major company is simply going to assume they'll have their job for another 10, 15, or 20 years (until they retire) and that they'll continue making $150,000 or more, based on the promotion they expect, inflation adjustments, and so on.

They may have been working for this company for 15 or 20 years already, having invested so much of their life in making sure it's successful. They have this false idea that because of their commitment to this company, the executive leadership is going to care about them if financial struggles become a reality for the company. Making those assumptions is certainly comfortable, but no one knows what tomorrow will bring. You could be working for Apple, have a decent upper mid-level management position, feel integral to the operations, and find yourself looking for a new job in just a couple of years. Over my 25 years, I've witnessed this with my clients over and over and over again.

It breaks my heart to see good people count so heavily on their employer for future financial security only to have the rug ripped out from under their feet when it's too late for a do-over. A pension, a company retirement plan, company stock, or their income – losing any of these (or all) can be devastating. There's no guarantee it will all still be there by the time they're in their 60s and ready to enjoy their retirement. With flexible working becoming a greater and greater asset to companies, they're firing full-time staff and turning toward freelancers and temporary workers more than ever.

Earlier, I briefly touched on the dire status of the pension systems run by state and local governments. It isn't any different with corporate pension plans. It's my assertion that this pension crisis, both government and corporate, is the 800-pound gorilla that will be the next major shoe to drop and no one's talking *seriously* enough about it. It's amazing to think very few people have acknowledged this pending disaster.

Pensions are the largest pool of assets in America and are the primary source for retirement income for millions of individuals, and a majority of them are underfunded. Yet this subject is ignored. It's absolute lunacy. It's beyond scary and should concern everyone – *especially those of you who are relying on it.*

Even the strongest companies won't survive forever. K-Mart was an unstoppable force once upon a time. So were Sears, Toys "R" Us, Comp USA, JC Penney, Kodak, Pan Am … remember them? Down the road from where I live, Payless Shoes just closed their doors. There will always be another Apple, Walmart, Home Depot, or Amazon busting through the ranks, doing things differently, and putting pressure on other former titans of the past. The new, hip company will become a dinosaur. It's not a question of *if*. It's only a question of *when*.

"But they can't touch my pension," is a comment I hear all the time.
Not true.
"But it was negotiated fairly. It's a legal contract. They agreed!"
Unfortunately, that doesn't matter.

If a company dissolves, if it goes out of business, what happens to the pensions? If they weren't protected or funded from the beginning, they're as good as promises written on Post-It notes: "The company must remain in business in order to continue funding the plan for current and future retirees." Yes, there's the PBGC (Pension Benefit Guarantee Corporation), which steps in when pension plans go under – but their responsibility is to help minimize the damage, not restore what was lost.

Luke and Sue counted on the company to take care of them. They expected the pension to be there, without question. Many state workers are doing the same thing right now, but most of the pensions are massively underfunded. It's like a pyramid scheme or shell game.

The writing's on the wall: millions of people are about to reach retirement only to find what they expected to receive is simply not going to be there, or it'll be drastically cut. It doesn't matter what the contract states. You cannot create money out of thin air.

> **Millions of people are about to reach retirement only to find what they expected to receive is simply not going to be there, or it'll be drastically cut**

What people need to realize is that we can no longer operate as we once did. From fluctuating 401(k) plans to the uncertainty of Social Security and pension plans to the lack of job security to an economy that shifts based on who's in power, to the ever growing shift towards automation, the paradigm has radically changed. We can no longer just follow simple guidelines to achieve financial peace of mind. Years ago, we had stable markets that we trusted, interest rates that were more favorable for savers and retirees, and a cost of living that was much lower (consider costs of healthcare, education, fuel, and housing). Today, markets are volatile, interest rates are at historic lows, pensions and social security are no longer assurances, and the cost of living is growing. This new paradigm will affect everyone regardless of his or her financial situation.

Despite my best efforts, I couldn't manage to convince Luke and Sue to take a greater percentage of their income and invest it safely for retirement. Sue got upset any time I would mention the fact they were carrying three enormous mortgages. She wanted to take *Action* based on her desires or hunches rather than on sound financial advice.

But how could she know that everything about Luke's job and company wasn't going to be fine?

What often happens when people begin increasing their income, especially significantly, is that they breathe a sigh of relief. They feel the weight of stress from just struggling paycheck to paycheck suddenly lifting from them. Unfortunately, that can lead to a devastating false sense of reality and financial security. That deep breath often leads to chasing material possessions they've always wanted to have. They can suddenly justify those expenses.

Luke and Sue got a taste of the good life and shifted gears as their belief system and structure changed. They were making enough money now that they could buy whatever they wanted, and their spending wasn't going to make a difference because the money was going to continue coming in. What an amazing belief system to build their financial future on! Instead of being relatively conservative with their investments, they started drooling at the stories they found in financial magazines in local newspapers about people who were making it rich in the dot-com age. But how much would be enough?

The *Results* of persisting in the idea that your company will take care of you – as Luke and Sue and thousands of others have discovered – can be losing almost everything you have. Too many times in my experience, this false sense of reality has resulted in devastating consequences that can be almost impossible to overcome at any age, particularly at 60 and beyond.

GETTING CAUGHT

 Beliefs: My company will take care of me. You followed what you were taught in school: Go to school, get good grades, get a job, buy a house, and after 40 years retire happily on your pension or your 401(k). You spend years working late nights and weekends and devoting your energy to your employer. You're driven to do a good job and you want your company to succeed. "I'll take care of you, and you'll take care of me" is the mindset we often have, but companies are focused more on their bottom line. If they make bad investments, decisions, or business choices, the employees often take the first and hardest hit.

 Excuses: "As long as I have my job, I'll be just fine." Instead of focusing on establishing a solid retirement portfolio of their own or creating alternative sources of income, many people get so comfortable in their company's past history, current status in the marketplace, or future prospects, that they feel confident their retirement funds will be available when they retire. This applies to government employees as well.

 Actions: Not planning for the "what-if" scenarios and taking unnecessary risks thinking nothing can go wrong. When things start to go sour, many people dig in deeper because they've put 100 percent of their faith in the company or organization they work for, still counting on what their employer has promised (never accepting that promises are cheap but delivering on them is never guaranteed).

Results: Realizing that perfect storms do occur and discovering too late that everything you counted on could very well be an illusion. When we put too much faith and reliance in our company's ability to honor its monetary obligations, we ignore the need to plan for the unforeseen and we find ourselves stuck, stranded in the middle of the woods with a bear trap dug right into our ankle.

I tell all my clients repeatedly that they need to begin planning for their future as though they won't have their job until retirement. Because, honestly, in today's economic climate, there may not be a retirement fund awaiting them when they retire.

It's wonderful when you're able to keep a position, get a promotion, and retire from the same company you've been working for over the past 30 or 40 years, but in modern America, that is the exception now rather than the rule. Your finances are most stable when they're firmly in your control and you're not reliant on one source of income to sustain you.

You may very well work for a great company that truly takes care of its employees, and if that's the case, better for you. That doesn't mean you should make unwise decisions when you're making good money.

Keep focused on the end goal: become self-reliant in your retirement years.

 YOUR TURN
Let's take another look at your life. Keep things in perspective. Pull out your guidebook and complete Activity #13.

This is another opportunity to begin diving deep down to the roots and see how your beliefs are impacting your financial life.

PART THREE

TIME

— TO —

TRANSFORM

My Story: Going Home

It's late summer. The temperatures in Minnesota are beginning to relent after nearly six straight weeks of high heat and humidity. My back aches and my muscles are sore, but I'm so much stronger. The work has been grueling and soon I'll be returning home to my parents, school, and friends.

I'll be getting back into football, and that's exciting. As I stand by the fence, having just completed one more coat of paint – another year, another few dollars in my account – I scan the farmland. The fence looks amazing. For now, anyway. A crow has landed on one of the posts about 25 feet away. He looks around and spots me. I gaze back, not upset, not worried, just observing.

As the years have progressed, I'm feeling the weight of life beginning to press in. A teenager is often told, "Don't worry about growing up too fast."

I don't. I haven't.

Yet what has moved from the distant backdrop of my mind to the forefront is beginning to take shape. I stand there, leaning against last month's initial work on this fence, confident that the paint there has long since dried. This project wraps around the entire farm. A homesick feeling overwhelms me.

I'm torn between two worlds: the one I live here and the one back home. The one where I'm a teenager, excited about football, hanging out with friends, perhaps meeting a special girl and going on a few dates. The life where I've gained so much knowledge that will help me prepare for life beyond high school and college.

I can't possibly fathom all the lessons I've learned here, not in this moment, not at this age, but I still feel the value of these precious summers spent in Minnesota with my grandparents.

Someday, perhaps 30 years into the future, I might have something to impart to my own children, friends, or others. I see this crow as wisdom. That's why he's staring at me; he's letting me know something special has happened here, something I couldn't have gained elsewhere – not with the education system in America, not through all the finance classes in college, and not for the first years in my journey to become a financial advisor.

Sometimes the foundations we build aren't laid by us. In fact, most of the time those stones are tossed down by other people, experiences, and information. I could have been told all these stories about my grandparents, been regaled about their stingy spending habits, their focus on saving, their reusing the bread from the toaster, and their getting upset when a kid ordered a lunch that was $2 more than the basic soup and sandwich.

Would those stories have meant the same thing to me?

Of course not. That's why the 16-year-old boy is leaning against that fence post, not satisfied with his work, effort, or money, but rather wishing these moments didn't have to end just yet.

In a few days, that young boy will fly home. That young boy will experience a true homesick, heartbreaking feeling, wondering at 16 if he will ever quite have this experience to live over again. In two years, he will be focused on college entrances, getting ready for the next chapter in his life, and won't likely spend another summer on this farm in Minnesota. Maybe he'll return for a week or two, but it won't be the same.

In a year, that boy is going to transition from relying on Mom and Dad for rides to obtaining his own driver's license, saving up to purchase his first automobile – a 1970 beater that will have long since seen better days. In two years, that boy will begin slipping away from the heartfelt lessons of his grandparents, but it will only be temporary. He will be, after all, what one may call a typical teenager, going to the movies, heading to the beach, going on dates, and basically practicing for adulthood.

When that boy heads off to college, he will get trapped by credit card debt, that feeling of having "free money" suddenly at his disposal. But somewhere along the line, all of these wonderful experiences in Minnesota will begin surrounding him, beginning to click into place.

In the years to come they will start to take shape and forge a new idea. We are shaped by our belief systems, which are shaped by our experiences, which can be influenced by family, friends, teachers, coaches, television, and the Internet. However, all that information alone can't produce change.

True change can occur only when a person is able to acknowledge how their *Beliefs* mold their *Excuses*, which manipulate their **Actions**; that opens the avenue to a sincere desire to make a change for better **Results**.

When I start each day to carry on my own personal mission, I am inspired. For a number of years I had lost my way. I just didn't have the passion I once had for this financial industry. I know now that what was missing was a truly transformative opportunity for myself and people the world over because of what I've learned in my career.

When I wake up with purpose, meaning, and a sincere desire to get my feet pounding on the ground and moving toward my goal of transforming the world's relationship with money, it inspires me. I feel fulfilled, which means every day is its own reward.

> **True change can occur only when a person is able to acknowledge how their *Beliefs* mold their *Excuses*, which manipulate their *Actions*; that opens the avenue to a sincere desire to make a change for better *Results*.**

My grandfather and grandmother taught me that rewarding yourself is just fine, but first you need to understand your financial situation to ensure you're not hurting yourself in the short or long run. This helped provide confidence that when I was truly pursuing something I was born to do, something I sincerely care about, I wouldn't be working another day in my life.

Many of the *Beliefs* we hold onto throughout life are established in our youth. How we observe our parents behaving, how they spent or saved money, can influence us for decades to come. Some of the lessons we learned out of high school, in college, or when we first joined the workforce can lay the foundation for how we act and behave when we start making money in the future.

I found myself journeying back to those Minnesota farm days, those wonderful summers spent with my grandparents, when I began trying to fully understand why my own clients were having such a difficult time making necessary changes in their approach to finances.

For a while they would make adjustments and things would improve, but like many people, they kept falling back.

Sometimes we just have to go back home. Sometimes we just have to go back and discover why we act the way we do about money. Sometimes we have to rewind our mindset, begin discovering what established our *Belief* systems, and begin to rewire our thinking. We have to be honest with ourselves because once we're honest, that's the starting point.

If you see yourself in any of these stories, if you see a pattern developing that could harm your financial future, I encourage you to dig deep into those harmful beliefs and explore what life could be like when you're no longer bound by that trap.

Return home.

YOUR TURN

It's time for personal reflection. Go to your guidebook and complete Activity #14. At this point in the journey, you'll certainly have more insights to consider.

CHAPTER 17

It's Time to Transform Your Destiny

Beliefs. What does the word mean, really? Merriam-Webster defines *belief* as *"a state or habit of mind in which trust or confidence is placed on some person or thing."*

Let's focus on the word habit for a moment. What is that? Again, Merriam-Webster defines *habit* as *"a settled tendency or usual manner of behavior."*

Our beliefs are formed and forged at an early age. They're tested and reshaped as we develop throughout our teenage years. They stretch and grow as we head off to college to enter the workforce, when we begin dating, when we begin discovering our identity, and as we move through life.

Some of our beliefs alter as we discover new things, learn new truths, or begin to look outside ourselves for answers, support, and help.

The longer we hold onto a firm belief system, the more likely it will lead to habitual behaviors. Then, the decisions and focus we have in life will begin to ride along on those beliefs without a second thought.

Have you ever noticed a particular habit you developed (maybe even without realizing it) and despite your best effort, it wouldn't abate? Maybe it was a habit of twiddling with your fingers while on the phone. Perhaps you started humming to yourself when nervous, such as when riding the subway home from work. I used to crack my knuckles, and it was exacerbated when I faced the prospect of speaking in front of a group of people.

Once you recognize the habit and want to change or stop it, what happens? It gets really hard to do, doesn't it?

Even with a plethora of information indicating the harm we might experience, bad habits are often tough to break.

It's difficult to shatter the habit. But *only* when we can begin chiseling away at that stubborn rock will we be able to start altering the belief upon which it's grounded.

Think of it like liquid concrete mix being spilled in the middle of a windy road. It hardens and soon becomes a hazard. Maybe you drive that same road every day, to and from work, to the store, to pick up your kids from practice, and so forth. You may first notice the spill and worm around it, but eventually as the street gets busier and busier, you either have to wait or slow down and deal with it.

In time, you become so used to that annoyance that you begin ignoring it, only slightly slowing down to avoid slamming your shocks too hard and jolting your whole body.

Do this long enough and your car will begin experiencing problems. You'll have to replace the shocks and struts sooner than you wanted. The brakes might wear out quicker. You'll probably discover ball joint failures, alignment issues, and even the tie-rods starting to break down.

All of these problems can lead to very serious safety issues on the road. You may simply decide to trade your car in for a newer, safer model, but what about your life?

What about your finances?

We don't just get to restart the game, so to speak. This is why understanding and acknowledging our belief systems are so important in helping us shape and reshape them into something that will protect us financially ... for the present and the future.

Everything we've talked about in the B.E.A.R. Trap is rooted in the foundation of our beliefs. The B.E.A.R. Trap is our *Beliefs*, *Excuses*, *Actions*, and *Results*.

If our ***Beliefs*** are poorly formed, faulty, or misguided (based on bad or nonexistent information, education, training, etc.), then we will begin developing excuses to move forward with specific actions that might lead to unwanted or unexpected results.

In order to keep doing (or pursuing) those things – whether it's a job, new business, bigger house, new car, circle of friends, etc. – we develop ***Excuses***.

Ever ask a young child why he knocked the vase over? "I didn't do it" or "It was already like that" might be their answer. Ask the same child why he didn't do his homework, and you'll find a wide range of answers.

Excuses.

When we want or don't want to do something, when we desire to purchase an item, or we strive after things our family or friends might not understand or agree with, we have a tendency to build up an army of excuses for continuing on those paths.

These excuses allow us to ***justify*** our next step … our **Actions**.

Buying the new house because we convinced ourselves we needed it. Switching from a decent job to a new one for more money and because we assume it'll launch us up that success ladder faster (even though ***now*** we have no seniority or reputation). Been there and done that myself, regrettably. Snagging the overpriced car or truck we'll never come close to using as it was fully designed. Throwing money at so-called investment or business opportunities more because we want to be accepted rather than them being sound financial opportunities.

If our actions are faulty and based on negative belief systems, they can and often do lead to unexpected and undesired **Results**.

The **Results** we end up with when we have the wrong belief systems in place will invariably turn out negatively.

It's a structure or pattern that builds one upon the other leading to losing savings, our house, our car, our family, our future possibilities.

And this all begins at that first letter, that first step … our **Beliefs**.

A good friend once mentioned that information doesn't cause transformation. We have access to more information than any other time in the history of the planet, but our financial decisions have (for the most part) only grown worse.

Go to any major bookstore and stroll down the business or finance sections and you'll find shelves of books packed with information. People gobble them up and make some minor changes in their outlook, viewpoints, and processes, but those usually only last a few months at best.

That's because what we need to do in order to make lasting, effective change is to transform our belief systems.

If we want true, lasting change to lead us into financial prosperity, security, and wealth, we need to infuse ourselves with the right mindset and an effective process that will transform our beliefs.

When we can achieve that, we won't need to chase after overnight riches, scour the horizon every day hoping to catch that one flicker of evidence that a new investment is going to multiply our portfolio a hundredfold, or seek anyone else's approval.

> If we want true, lasting change to lead us into financial prosperity, security, and wealth, we need to infuse ourselves with the right mindset and an effective process that will transform our beliefs.

With the right belief set, we'll understand how to care for the money we earn, be patient and develop the right plan, and avoid the common trappings that infiltrate every corner of our lives in modern times.

I have other stories that I may share in an updated version of this book. But I will say, the underlying cause of each one is the same.

Your beliefs will shape every decision you make. Are they wired for success? I encourage you to discover how to enjoy true financial peace and avoid the struggles, pitfalls, and failures you just read about here.

WELL? ARE YOU READY?

It's time to make the next move. I know you're ready. You've proven it by reading to this point.

You understand the challenges. You see the problems. You likely related to many of the harmful Beliefs you read about. They surround you each day.

You've seen yourself in these words. You've felt the same pains, the same struggles, the same fears.

And I'm sure you've come to some similar conclusions: information is readily available and – by itself – **it *has done nothing to help*.**

I encourage you to head over to www.johnmacgregor.net and see what a truly transformational program can offer.

You'll find powerful resources, including information about *ThrivePath*, a revolutionary solution to people's financial freedom and peace of mind.

ThrivePath is a paradigm shift that offers a blueprint to the millions of people around the world who are living paycheck to paycheck and struggling with financial stress and anxiety. This proven process is designed for all who are looking to transform their relationship with money so that they may forever live a life of financial peace, freedom and joy.

For the first time, we have blended the latest in neurological and genetic research with 25 years of hands-on financial advice, to understand and solve how people can actually transform their relationship with money so they can live the life they deserve to live.

ThrivePath is a simple to follow, online seven-step neurologically based process we guide you through. This process is scientifically designed for people who are looking to go from financial pain to financial peace, in a manner of self-discovery, self-awareness, and joy.

This program yields far bigger outcomes than more money in your bank account. It was developed to change people's lives forever.

YOUR TURN
Let's wrap this all up in the guidebook. Head over to Activity #15. It's been a great journey with you. I'm proud of you. Once you complete the activity, I'll see you back here.

WHERE DO WE GO FROM HERE?

As mentioned at the end of Chapter 2, I encourage you to seek out the ThrivePath Personal Assessment. If you haven't already done so, I would advocate that you explore this powerful personal assessment.

This personal assessment was specifically designed to see precisely where you are on the spectrum of being *Wired to Be Rich*. Go through it and answer 20 quick and easy questions. You'll get a FREE personal assessment of your current financial situation in order to help you determine which PATH is perfect for you. As I've always said, If you don't know where you are, you'll *never* get to where you want to be.

> **If you don't know where you are, you'll *never* get to where you want to be.**

In fact, if you took the assessment when you began this book, I would recommend you take it again. Now that you've gone this far, your answers to those questions and your results may be surprisingly different.

I'm really excited that you get to take this journey.

When you get to this point, I *know* you're ready for something more, something better.

ThrivePath offers you the guidance you need.

No matter where you were headed, no matter how far off course you slipped, it's not too late to change.

I promise you that.

What we've discovered while developing and launching ThrivePath, and since helping so many men and women already, is that you're closer than you think to living a life of *true*, lasting financial peace, joy, and fulfillment.

The greatest power a person possesses is the power to *choose*. ThrivePath can and will serve as the perfect bridge to close that gap between where people are now and where they *choose* to be – no matter how big that gap is.

Your financial future is not a matter of chance. It's a matter of choice. It is not a thing to be waited for; it is something to be embraced.

Here's to your next, best chapter of your financial life. Here's to your new future.

I wish you all the best!

–John MacGregor

P.S. I would love to hear from you! Please send me your comments and especially your success stories: hello@johnmacgregor.net

John MacGregor

- Founder & CEO, ThrivePath, LLC
- CFP® – CERTIFIED FINANCIAL PLANNER™
- International Speaker
- Author, *Unlock Your Money Code* and *The Top 10 Reasons the Rich Go Broke*

John has been a leader and innovator in the financial services industry for over 25 years. John's passion is helping people understand how easy it is to live a financially secure life if they have the right mindset and process in place.

Over the years he has helped thousands upon thousands of individuals create successful financial futures through his distinctive methods and systems. His unique proven approach to creating financial security, which he developed, has made him a highly demanded media personality. His paradigm-shifting brain-based financial system not only addresses the specific knowledge and tools one needs to have a secure financial platform, it is also designed to help people become highly aware of the road blocks that have stopped them from doing "The Next Right Thing" in their financial lives.

Uniquely, John has held a variety of positions within the financial services industry and is able to bring a broad vantage point to the reader. From Financial Advisor, Complex Manager, Financial Advisor Coach and Trainer, Institutional Sales Director, Pension Consulting, and National Sales Leader, John has seen this business from multiple angles and offers insight you will not find in any other financial transformation book or accompanying process.

John has also trained and coached thousands of Financial Advisors in how to more successfully assist their clients with their financial management needs. He shares his experience and exclusive systems with advisors who are facing the many challenges of today's complex and uncertain marketplace.

John has been recognized as one of the top financial planners in the nation by The Consumer Research Council and one of the most influential in the retirement industry by The Boston Research Group. In addition, American businessman, investor, and Best-selling author, Robert Kiyosaki, who has sold over 100 million books in his *Rich Dad* financial series, has labeled John: "My 'expert' advisor on the very important world of financial planning."

Visit: johnmacgregor.net

RESOURCES

*Get the support you need on your journey
to financial freedom and peace of mind!*

The Top 10 Reasons The Rich Go Broke
Supplemental Guidebook

Your "Wired To Be Rich" Personal Assessment:
Your Journey to Financial Freedom and Peace of Mind Begins HERE

Free White Paper:
"The Ultimate Guide to Selecting Your Financial Advisor"

Free eBook:
"Unlock Your Money Code: Master Your Mind and Live Your Rich Life"

The Think & Transform Guided Manifestation:
The "Mind Over Money" Guided Visualization Program to Financial
Freedom and Peace of Mind. Sit, relax and discover who you can and
will become

*For these resources and additional information,
and to connect to a community of like-minded individuals,
please join us by visiting*

JOHNMACGREGOR.NET